Killing the Victim before
the Victim Kills You

Establishing Responsible Relationships
through Making and Keeping Promises

Derek M. Watson
Daniel L. Tocchini
Larry Pinci

Mashiyach Press

Killing the Victim Before the Victim Kills You
Copyright © 1996, by Derek M. Watson, Daniel L. Tocchini, and Larry Pinci.

Requests for information should be addressed to:
Mashiyach Press
1055 West College Avenue, #286
Santa Rosa, CA 95401

Publisher's Cataloguing-in-Publication Data

Watson, Derek McCollum
Killing the Victim before the Victim Kills You: Establishing Responsible Relationships through Making and Keeping Promises / by Derek M. Watson, Daniel L. Tocchini, and Larry Pinci.
p. cm.
Includes bibliographical references and index.
ISBN 1-888896-02-7 : $16.95
1. Christian Life 2. Promises—Religious aspects—Christianity 3. Interpersonal relations I. Tocchini, Daniel L. 1955-   . II. Pinci, Larry, 1960-   . III. Title.

Library of Congress Catalogue Card Number: 96-83941

All rights reserved. No part of this book may be used or reproduced, stored in a retrieval system, or transmitted in any form or by any means—electronic, mechanical, photocopy, recording, or any other—without the prior permission of the publisher, except for brief quotations in printed reviews.

All Scripture quotations, unless otherwise indicated, are taken from the *New American Standard Bible*. Copyright © The Lockman Foundation, 1960, 1962, 1963, 1986, 1971, 1972, 1973. Used by permission.

Cover Designed by Carla White and Bob Payne
Edited by Stanley Reahard

Printed in the United States of America.
96 97 98 99 00 / 10 9 8 7 6 5 4 3 2 1

If we had forgotten the name of our God, or extended our hands to a strange god; Would not God find this out? For He knows the secrets of the heart. But for Thy sake we are killed all day long; we are considered as sheep to be slaughtered.

Psalm 44:20-22

Table of Contents

Acknowledgments

Every ministry's success is the result of the hard work and dedication of its supporters. Mashiyach is no exception. Many people have poured their hearts and souls out to realize their vision for transformation of heart and character.

From the very start of this work, our sponsors around the country have been the arms and legs; nothing happens without them! Our gratitude, thanks, and prayers go to them and their families: Victor and Stephanie Barnard, Gary Bolen, Brent and Joanne Brody, Scott and Jude Carriker, Lee Anne Carrothers, David and Lorrie Cleveland, Gloria Compatore, Gary and Kim Cordery, Dave and Carol Demars, Dave and Caren Dillman, Bernard and Sandra Dupliessis, Lawrence and Valerie Edwards, Grace Esclamado and Ehrhardt Groothoff, Rick Frey, Ann Gilbert, Darin Gilchriese, Anita Gilmore, Sam and Miriam Golden, Mark and Karen Graeser, Tom and Chris Heermans, Gary and Kaye Hensen, Pamela Keohohou, David and Tina Larsen, Richard and Sonja Larsen, John Lynn, Henry and Tina Malone, Ricki and Tina May, Mike and Carrie Matheny, Gary and Sue Metz, Al and Chris Minott, Tom and Molly Moore, Steve and Kelly Munro, Don and Pam Owen, Randy and Kathy Ann Peugh, John and Laura Pezzi, Scott and Trice Pfeiffer, Julie Pinci, Michael and Tamie Platt, Bo and Stanley Reahard, Pat and Kathy Reece, Larry and Beverly Reed, Mark and Marsha Robbins, John Schoenheit, Kevin and B.J. Smith, Dan and Mary Stockemer, Joseph Stone, Aileen Tocchini, Tony and Jane Tuck, Hank and Linda Vance, Tonya Wann, Laurie Watson, Jerry and Pat Westfall, and finally our peripatetic sponsors-at-large, Peter and Diane Woolley.

In addition to our sponsors, many others have contributed themselves to the vision of Mashiyach Ministries. To all of our faithful friends and stalwart co-workers, thanks to you all: Sherman and Linda Brees, Bill and Cachy Brister, Linda Cavalli, Andy and Linda Costa, Rick and Jenny Davis, Warren and Linda Goolsby, Koinonia Foster Homes, Jon and Sharon Illg, Leon Indart, Debby Katz, Bill and Laurie Kellas, Paul and Teri Looney, Ken and Julia McGrath, Bob and Judy Mumford, Mike and Kathy Nunes, Barry and Sheila Pfaehler, Will Pilcher, Stephen Rogers, Marci Ross, Ed and Wanda Ryborz, Bill and Jenny Shattuck, Jack Watson and Nimbus Partners, Dave and Sherry Wesson, and Steve and Lisa Young.

Special thanks to Colonel and Miriam Doner, without whom Momentus would have been a short-lived experiment.

This book has benefited enormously from the input of a largely volunteer band. Our thanks and gratitude go to Steve Marshall who helped reorganize the flow of our thoughts throughout. Thanks, too, to Jeannette Destruel Tocchini for her comments on the Introduction and first chapter.

Special thanks to Dr. Monte Wilson, guardian of orthodoxy, and Edward Kavanaugh, educator *par excellence*, for reading the manuscript and offering many helpful suggestions.

Freedom Patriots Press has been blessed by the creative input of Tim and Carla White and the faithful service of our friend, Greg Stockton.

Our tireless and brilliant editor, Stanley Reahard, deserves accolades for her ability to extract the precious from the vile; without Stanley, this work would be a shadow of what it has become. Special thanks go to Suzanne Snyder for her attention to detail in editing, proof-reading, and indexing the manuscript.

The impact of some individuals has been so profound in our lives that they stand in a class by themselves. John P.

Hanley is one such individual. Thank you John for your stand for transformation and passion, and for your stalwart guidance through the years. Our hats also are doffed to Jim Hellam, Ray Blanchard, and Charlie Bloom—men whose wisdom and insight into the human soul continue to amaze and humble us.

Our lives would not be the same without the wisdom, love, guidance, and stability of our pastors: Father Paul and Anita Edwards, Father Rob and Cindy Bethancourt, both of Emmanuel Episcopal Church; and J.R. and JoAnne Young of the Santa Rosa Christian Church.

Finally, our hearts have been cleansed by the love of all the participants of *Momentus*, *One Accord*, and *Legacy*: You each are a gift from God.

Preface

The principles and truths we expound here are similar to all of God's truths: like gravity, they work for all, regardless of creed. Establishing responsible relationships works for Christians and non-Christians alike. We endeavor here to provoke a transformation from loving self first to loving God and others first. This book is meant for the individual, because it is the individual who turns the world inside out—not a government, not a religion, and not a philosophy. It is not written to be an answer, but to spur an inquiry designed to provoke the victim in each of us to yield to a vision bigger than himself or herself—a vision of building a cathedral out of his or her life for the glory of God and the benefit of others; and in the process of inquiring, to actually become a victor.

For those committed to making a recipe of their life with God and others, for those who reduce life to a list of "to do's," this book may become another bone to throw into the pot—another philosophy, theology, or psychology that will confirm their inability to live as victors. We have written this book for those who listen to more than their own voice, who think of more than their own image, and who love more than their own pleasure. We have written this book for those who dare to build cathedrals in the midst of housing tracts, who see beyond the immediate horizon, and who are willing to risk themselves for a future worth having. We have written this book for those who choose to be victors.

A note on language:

Collaborating on a book poses challenges that a solitary author does not face. One of these is the use of pronouns. Through this book, we will use the collective pronouns "we," "our" and "us" to refer to all of us—the whole human race. In certain instances (this being one of them), we will use "we," "our," and "us" to refer to the three of us. Otherwise, we will use the personal pronouns "I," "me," and "my" to represent our voice as authors. In ambiguous instances we will add clarifying parenthetical statements.

Another problem all writers face is the use of the masculine personal pronoun to represent an indefinite individual. We have decided to use both the masculine and feminine singular pronouns on an alternating basis to represent the indefinite usage.

Finally, we have included stories, vignettes, and examples of interactions with people from our work in the *Momentus* training.* In most cases we have disguised and created composite incidents. For those that are retold directly, we have received permission from the people involved.

Derek M. Watson
Daniel L. Tocchini
Larry Pinci

Santa Rosa, CA

Momentus is a four-day experiential learning environment designed to allow participants to discover and realign the belief systems that govern their lives. One of the major belief systems that govern many people is that of being a victim.

Introduction

Inside of each of us lives a victim.

The victim complains, threatens, moans, and—most of all—shifts the blame by pointing the finger at others, circumstances, and even God. The victim inside rebels at the idea that whatever we reap, we must have sown.

This victim is relentless, waiting and watching for any opportunity to lay the blame for both the good and the bad in life on external circumstances, whether they be situations or people. Being a victim is a way of relating to people and events around us that surrenders the control of our lives to others.

Whenever we refuse to govern ourselves; whenever we refuse to take responsibility for ourselves and our vision; whenever we abdicate our God-given place to govern ourselves, we surrender our power to determine our destiny—our power to be victors. By default we become victims.

The result of giving the victim room to govern our lives is death: the death of relationships, passion, joy, and peace. This victim must be continually put to death, or it *will* kill us.

How have you been a victim in the last hour, in the last day, in the last week? In the last month, how many times and how long have you languished as a victim, losing the ground you had previously taken toward your vision of the future?

To see the space we give the victim in our lives, just turn on daytime television. From the plots of soap-operas to the parade of bizarre specimens that fill the swivel chairs of talk shows, we love to see and hear the victim play it up. Unfortunately, this broadcast caricature gives the rest of us "normal people" the cover to run our own victim scams.

We all experience the vulnerability of being a victim at times: the sense of being out of control; living a life dictated by circumstances, another person, fear, or even God. The question of "who or what is in control?" reveals the times and the places in our lives in which we live as victims. Like a stroke of lightening in a pitch-black night, this question illuminates the nightmarish impact of giving the victim a place in our lives.

This book challenges you to look at the impact that living as a victim has on all the relationships in your life. The impact is unequivocally negative. Living as a victim deadens the spirit, the soul, and the body. Living as a victim kills vision and results in a drab and despairing existence.

On the other hand, killing the victim in its many guises rekindles a life worth living. Even considering the question of who or what is in control may provoke the victim inside to rear its ugly head—perhaps by raising suspicions, or by ridicule, or by a yawn of boredom.

How you ask yourself this question and how you answer it are pivotal to your life. The importance of both will not diminish after you have finished the last chapter and laid this book aside. It takes a lifetime to fully answer the question of who or what is in control of your life.

Relating to God and others responsibly is the key to becoming more like Jesus and the essence of governing ourselves in the liberty of Christ. We have seen over and over again with the more than four thousand people who have participated in the *Momentus* training that living as a victim brings unnecessary pain and suffering in life, and stifles maturity in individuals, resulting in a stagnant and apathetic church.

Pain and suffering can by no means be eradicated in this life. It is, after all, in the crises of life that Christians have most powerfully witnessed the love of God to an unbelieving world. From the Christians who died in the Coliseum to Mother Theresa in Calcutta, these witnesses show the world a more powerful way of living than satisfying our immediate need for comfort. Their witness shows us the power of taking responsibility in life—investing their lives in a future worth living for, and if need be, worth dying for; a way of living that is so rewarding that these men and women are willing to sacrifice their lives to secure it for their family, friends, and themselves. They have found the pearl of great price.

In sharp contrast to the powerful witness of self-sacrificial love, the victim settles for the opposite—a powerless and ineffective life of despair and futility. The victim trades the short-term pain of resolving a crisis for the long, dull ache of hopelessness. Victims avoid the sharp pain that comes from living responsibly, because they have no vision bigger than themselves. For them, self-preservation and comfort become their only goal. They have no future worth suffering for; nothing worth the sacrifice of their lives; no pearl of great price, for which they would sell all that they own.

Like the grasshopper who spends its summer in wanton living with no vision of the coming winter, the victim is caught in the immediate. With no inkling of the rigors and risks of the coming winter, the grasshopper fritters away its time on its hobbies and amusements. In contrast, the ant diligently spends its summer gathering food for the long winter months. Putting aside hobbies and fun, or indulging them in measure, the ant prepares provisions for the winter—provisions that insure its survival and the continuation of its colony.

The struggle to live responsibly is every human's struggle. Every day we face this challenge and many times we lose the battle. Only one man has ever lived without committing the sin of relating to God, others, and Himself as a victim. Yet, Jesus of Nazareth was victimized by both the Roman and Jewish authorities when He was scourged, beaten, vilified, and crucified for crimes He did not commit. Nevertheless, regardless of how He was victimized, He was not a victim.

If anyone had a right to feel sorry for Himself and blame others, Jesus did! He did not seek the tortures He endured. Jesus did not go easily to the cross. In the garden of Gethsemane, He struggled with the choice between His will and the Father's will. He persevered and chose to complete the course He had promised His Father: to be the Lamb of God that takes away the sins of the world. Jesus' choice to forgive, even in the midst of the agony of the cross, shows His liberty from being a victim—only a victor can forgive.

What made Jesus different? How did He live without becoming a victim? What empowered Him to be a victor? These are burning questions for all of us who take His name and call ourselves Christians. If we are to be like Him, we need to know both *how* He is different and *what* made Him so.

The defining character of Christ as a victor, which supported His whole ministry, was the vision from which He lived—that of glorifying God by serving others. He found His vision fulfilled in other people, not in things. Nothing He did was frivolous or empty; He lived each moment with people to open up the possibility of greater life.

His preaching had power and authority (Matthew 21:23), because He taught a simple message—a repentance or *metanoia* ("change of mind" in Greek) from loving self to loving others; from knowing truths to being true; from being a victim to being a victor.

Wherever Jesus went, He challenged those around Him to change their lives. Think of the woman at the well (John 4:7-28). She met Jesus as He was resting while the disciples were off gathering food for a meal. Even at rest, when it would have been easy to pass up an opportunity, Jesus took the time to serve her and assist her in changing the course of her life. In the process of meeting Jesus, she experienced a *metanoia*—a complete change of heart. Never mind that He was tired and hungry. Never mind that He'd already put in a long day. Never mind that she was nothing but a despised Samaritan.

In the book of Luke, Jesus declares His vision for His public ministry:

> He came to Nazareth, where He had been brought up; and as was His custom, He entered the synagogue on the Sabbath, and stood up to read. And the book of the prophet Isaiah was handed to Him. And He opened the book and found the place where it was written, "The spirit of the Lord is upon me, because he has anointed me to preach the gospel to the poor. He has sent me to proclaim release to the captives, and recovery of sight to the blind, to set free those who are downtrodden, to proclaim the favorable year of the Lord (Luke 4:16-19).

This passage describes Jesus' vision in concrete terms; it describes the good news He brought to the woman at the well, the lepers, the tax-gatherers and sinners, and to us, if we receive Him.

Imagine what it was like for prisoners in Nazi concentration camps, when the Allied troops delivered them from captivity. What was it like to be set free from such crushing imprisonment? Yet this is nothing compared to what Jesus came to accomplish by preaching the gospel to the poor. Didn't Jesus come to turn us from our dependence on external resources to relying on the resources of the kingdom within? Wasn't His purpose to set us free to govern ourselves, to forsake the life of a victim and to live victoriously?

Responsibility, repentance, and vision are central to moving from being a victim to being a victor. In this book we will examine what these three concepts mean to you. We will not provide answers that will make you more certain in your knowledge about God or people. Rather, our purpose is to provide questions and assertions that will stimulate you to repent; to empower you to turn in trust to God, in the face of your lack of knowledge and understanding; to confront you with how often you engage life from a victim's stance; and to provoke you to be a victor. Only a victor can love and perform good deeds. Victims do not have the freedom for either.

Our purpose is that of Hebrews 10:24: "And let us consider how we may spur one another on toward love and good deeds." The word "spur" means "to prod with a sharp stick, to poke." Only through spurring one another can we enter whole-heartedly into what it is to love another as Christ loves us and turn from being a victim to being a victor.

1. Who or What is in Control?

*Like a city that is broken into and without walls is a man
who has no control over his spirit.*

Proverbs 25:28

Who or what is in control of your life?

Have you ever asked yourself this question?

Consider it. Ponder it. Who or what controls you? This is
not the kind of question that you can answer quickly and move
past. As it sinks into your soul, this question reveals the
attitude of your heart—how you relate to God, others,
circumstances, and yourself. This question reveals whether
you are living as a victim or as a victor. To bring this
revelation, however, you must be willing to examine your life
in detail. Those who struggle in the question of who or what
is in control will discover the minutia of their hearts.

If you are Christian, your immediate answer to who or
what controls you may be: "Why, God is of course. I gave my
life to him in 19xx when I was saved and He took control of it."
Perhaps you find that the act of questioning who is in control
of your life is unsettling; maybe even threatening. I know
every time I seriously consider it, tremors run through the
foundations of my life. I come up against the fear of
abandoning myself to a mysterious and almighty God. When
I ponder the thought of what controls my life, I realize how

little I actually surrender to God compared with my public confession. This question brings to the foreground everything in my life that I would prefer not to see, everything that I would be happier pretending not to know.

If you are not Christian, your answer to the question of who or what is in control may come with similar speed: "Why I am of course. I didn't just fall off of the turnip truck. If I don't take charge of my life, nobody else will." Here too, the speed with which you answer may belie the vulnerability you feel inside when you seriously entertain this question.

The extent of our ignorance about ourselves and what governs us is almost without bounds—as is the deceitfulness of our hearts at hiding it from us. I (Dan) recently came face to face with an enormous burden of bitterness and anger toward my younger brother, Leo. I never even realized I was carrying it until the day I "forgot" to send him a birthday present.

Now this may seem minor, but I always send Leo a gift on his birthday. He's the "baby" of the family and has always been very special to me. Of all my siblings, he was the one I felt closest to. So what was in control of my relationship with Leo that I would forget his birthday like that? I was sorely tempted to excuse myself. After all, I was extremely busy at the time with the ministry and family concerns; my mother-in-law had cancer, my wife needed me more than ever. Surely it was just the weight of everything else going on in my life that caused the lapse.

"But this is *Leo*," I thought, "your special brother, the one who calls you when he needs help, the one you always make time to go visit in Seattle, the one you can talk to about anything." No matter how hard I tried to excuse myself, questions about the motivation of my heart continued to nag me. Finally I forced myself to look honestly at our relationship and face the fact that it had begun to disintegrate.

Deep inside, I knew it had started about a year before when Leo called me to announce his engagement. I was thrilled with his news. He was full of wedding plans and bubbling over with excitement. It would have been impossible not to rejoice with him! Then he dropped a bombshell on me. He'd asked another minister to perform the ceremony instead of me. Not only that, he'd asked our brother, Corey, to be his best man. Would I consider speaking during the ceremony? Speaking? I was stunned. Not ask his own brother, an ordained minister, to perform the wedding? Apparently Leo didn't value our relationship as much as I did.

I felt betrayed. I went cold. Then I went right to being a victim. I swallowed my hurt (after all, victims don't want to "hurt anyone's feelings" by telling them the truth) and instead of telling him how I felt, I lied to my brother. In the most magnanimous voice I could muster, I said I did not mind a bit that he'd asked another minister instead of me. I then added a bit of revenge, while continuing to sound sincere. I said I'd really like to be there but I was already scheduled to lead a *Momentus* training that weekend so I couldn't possibly attend. I felt hollow inside when I hung up the phone, but still refused to look at the situation honestly. I buried myself in other "more pressing" work. I refused to look at who or what was in control of me at that moment. I didn't want to know if it was my love for my brother, my desire for his happiness, or the betrayal I felt about the wedding plans. Surely I could have rescheduled the training. But I never even considered the possibility, nor was I willing to look at the real reason behind my refusal to attend such a momentous occasion in my brother's life.

It was not until the forgotten birthday gift that I was finally able to enter the pain of his betrayal and see the wall of bitterness I had built up toward my beloved brother. Wild horses could not have kept me from picking up the phone and seeking forgiveness. God bless Leo. He forgave me; he always does. I may not be able to go back and enjoy that special time of blessing with my family at his wedding, but my willingness to finally confess my sin to my brother has opened the door to an even richer relationship than we had before.

This whole book hangs on the question of who or what is in control of your life. God has given you the authority and liberty to steward your life; whenever you surrender that control to someone or something else, you become a victim to that person or thing. This can even be true of how we relate to God. Instead of acting as responsible sons or daughters, we act as victims of His actions. How many Christians spend their lives waiting, hoping for a revelation from God as to what course of action to take? With the apparent lack of clear direction from God as an excuse for inaction, we allow ourselves to be God's victim.

This brings up some sticky wickets: Isn't God ultimately in control? Isn't the major task of the Christian walk that of surrendering control to God? How then is it possible to be a victim to God?

Our Christian vocabulary gets in our way here. We confuse *control* with *service*. The issue is not control, but rather whose will are we serving. Think of Jesus—He perfectly exercised His power of choice; He was never carried away by an excuse or circumstance. He freely chose to yield His will in favor of the Father's will.

My wife and I (Derek) occasionally lead the children's praise time at our Episcopal church. All the children in the service march out so that the parents can listen to the sermon and have a time of ministry in relative peace. One Sunday, we had 14 boys and girls between the ages of two and nine. If you think leading children's praise is a walk in the park, try it sometime. This Sunday, one of the nine-year-old boys, let's call him Mario, really got my goat. Within minutes, I found myself raging inside about this boy. I called him everything but a son of God! He was devious and underhanded, mean-spirited and emotionally disturbed. Time dragged on more and more slowly. I began to dread the next time I would have to run praise time with him in the group.

As I was preparing the obligatory snack and juice, plotting how to give Mario the smallest portions in order to exact revenge, I suddenly stopped. I realized that my whole internal state was being dictated by this nine-year-old boy. God pierced my soul and demanded a change of heart—Mario wasn't out to get me—he was merely a hurting and angry boy. I was astounded at how deeply I had slipped into being a victim to Mario's actions. In that flash of revelation, I was able to love him, whereas moments before I was ready to strangle him.

This example shows us how moment-by-moment we battle, fight, scratch, kick, and wrestle with the victim who lives in us. With love, diligence, discipline, and fortitude, we can weaken and perhaps even kill the victim inside before he kills us.

Both the Christian's and non-Christian's answers to the question of control are equally correct. The Christian can affirm that the Scriptures state clearly that Jesus is the author and finisher of our faith (Hebrews 5:9 and 12:2) and so He ultimately determines our eternal destiny. Even the lives of those who don't believe in Him are in His control, in that God has sovereign control of all creation. But the non-Christian's answer is also true: if you don't take action to have your life turn out according to your vision, nobody, including God, will make it happen for you. As Proverbs says, "Commit to the LORD whatever you do, and your plans will succeed. . . . In his heart a man plans his course, but the LORD determines his steps" (Proverbs 16:3, 9 NIV). Other scriptures, such as I Samuel 10:7 (in which the prophet Samuel encourages Saul to "do for yourself what the occasion requires; for God is with you"), point out the necessity of taking action based on our own vision of what is best.

The assumption that our actions ought to be based on our vision and dreams of the future does not generate much controversy either in the church or the world. In many self-help books, religious and otherwise, this principle is considered the key to a successful life. But in many of these books, questions about choosing a course of action operate on the level of tactics. A more powerful approach is to move to the level of strategy with the questions: 'For whom do you plan?' and 'To whom does your vision direct you?' These questions are just another way of asking, 'Whose will are you serving?'

Consider the question of who or what is in control apart from your theological, political, and philosophical convictions; apart from the way you *hope* your life is; and ponder who or what controls you in reality. What does the reality of how you live, the fruit of your day-to-day existence say about who or what controls you? How often do you shrink from someone because of past hurts or failures? How often do you refrain from acting because of your resentment or bitterness from past betrayals? How often do you determine what is possible for you and others based on the circumstances that surround you in the moment of decision? As you answer each of these questions, consider how you act. Every time you allow a past hurt, a failure, a feeling, or a circumstance to determine your life, you are relating to these incidents as a victim.

A Victim Defined

We have progressed to this point in this book without fully defining what we mean by the terms *victim* and *victor*. I will use Adam and Eve to describe victims and Jesus and Gideon as examples of victors. Identifying when we become a victim to others, circumstances, or ourselves is often a challenging and subtle task. But the simple definition is this: A victim allows his life to be governed by external circumstances, people, or events. Victims believe they have no choices—that they are powerless.

Let's look at the first victims recorded in the Bible—the familiar account of Adam and Eve from the third chapter of Genesis. After Adam and Eve ate the fruit from the tree of the knowledge of good and evil, they hid from God and covered their nakedness. When God finds them He asks:

> Have you eaten from the tree of which I commanded you not to eat?" And the man said, "The woman whom *Thou* gavest to be with me, she gave me from the tree, and I ate." Then the LORD God said to the woman, "What is this you have done?" And the woman said, "The serpent deceived me, and I ate." (Genesis 3:12, emphasis added.)

What interpretations were Adam and Eve making about reality and God that resulted in this victim stand?

In order to fall to Satan's temptation, Adam and Eve must have come to the conclusion that God had sent them into the world ill-equipped. If they had continued to believe the opposite—that in creating them in His image, God had given them everything pertaining to life and godliness, including dominion over all creation, even the serpent—they would not have fallen to the temptation that they needed something else in order to be like God.

Adam and Eve bought into the serpent's interpretation that God was withholding something from them—specifically the knowledge of good and evil—that would make them like God. Paradise contained everything for Adam and Eve to live the perfect human existence. Genesis 2:9 says that ". . . out of the ground the LORD God caused to grow every tree that is pleasing to the sight and good for food; the tree of life also in the midst of the garden, and the tree of the knowledge of good and evil." Every tree that was good to eat was in the garden. God provided for every physical and spiritual need, for sustenance and pleasure. He even gave them the tree of life to provide eternal life.

But why put the tree of the knowledge of good and evil in the garden? Is not this tree a big problem? A blight in an otherwise perfect setting? Why would God *do* that?

The tree of the knowledge of good and evil guaranteed Adam and Eve's freedom. Adam and Eve were not automatons; they were not puppets at the beck and call of the Great Puppeteer. They were created with the absolute ability and responsibility to choose. The tree of the knowledge of good and evil safeguarded their freedom.

Adam and Eve's freedom before the Fall was different from any that we will experience before Christ returns. They were in perfect communion with God, they were naked and were not ashamed—without the knowledge of sin and without the taint of disobedience. The freedom we experience is entirely different. We are equally free to choose whatever we will, but we choose from the perspective of already knowing evil and being slaves of an evil kingdom. Adam and Eve knew no sin before the Fall, but could and did choose disobedience.

Saying that the tree of the knowledge of good and evil safeguarded Adam and Eve's freedom does not tell us what that tree actually represented.

We can begin with what it was not. The tree of the knowledge of good and evil was not set in the garden to teach Adam and Eve right from wrong. Adam and Eve already knew what was right and what was wrong, before they ate of the fruit. God created them as moral beings with a conscience.

Learning right from wrong was not the result of eating the fruit.

Eating the fruit of this tree completed their shift from focusing on God and creation to focusing on themselves. With themselves as the center of attention, Adam and Eve realized they were naked and became afraid. The serpent's temptation was for Adam and Eve to regard themselves as independent and separate from God—to view God with suspicion. However this was not a *result* of eating the fruit, it was the cause. Later, God says, "Behold, the man has become like one of Us, knowing good and evil" (Genesis 3:22). This was the reason Adam and Eve were banished from the Garden, lest they eat from the tree of life and live forever. God, although self-aware, is not self-focused. Becoming self-focused therefore is not what God refers to in the comment "the man has become like Us."

So how *did* Adam and Eve become like God by eating the fruit? The act of eating the fruit was an assertion of their own authority to measure right and wrong. By eating the fruit, Adam and Eve set their own standard of good and evil. This inclination runs deep within the human heart. It is the power that has rationalized the greatest evils in the history of man. By eating the forbidden fruit, Adam and Eve asserted their own standards and ignored God's standard.

This right to declare what is good and what is evil is the province of God alone. The human race usurped the throne and assumed the role that is only God's.

The tree, therefore, represented Adam and Eve's obedience and submission to God's reign. In deciding to eat from the tree of the knowledge of good and evil, Eve and Adam both usurped God's role and became victims. We have defined a victim as someone whose life is governed by external circumstances, people, or events. In contrast, the victor governs himself by his vision and promises. Circumstances on the one hand and vision on the other are not mutually exclusive. In the next chapter we will examine the relationship between the two.

Adam and Eve were victims to the external circumstance of the temptation of the serpent. The decision to eat was the "trip" that started the Fall. The false reality spun by the serpent around the tree of the knowledge of good and evil—that it represented God's withholding from Adam and Eve, that He had made them second-class citizens, and that God's blessing was really a curse—governed their lives and their choices, rather than God's statement that "God saw all that He had made, and behold, it was very good" (Genesis 1:31).

In buying into the serpent's interpretation of reality instead of God's, Adam and Eve entered fully into victimhood. They then compounded their error by blame-shifting—pointing the finger at someone else as the reason for their actions. Adam pointed at Eve (and ultimately God who had given him Eve). Eve blamed the serpent. Their answers to God only confirmed what was already apparent. Adam and Eve chose to be victims by eating the forbidden fruit, and then continued in their victimhood by being unrepentant and blame shifting.

What is a Victor?

In contrast, Gideon is an example of a victor, although he is from a different mold than our usual superhero. Gideon was the quintessential underdog. He was the youngest boy in the lowest family of the smallest tribe of Israel. He was threshing wheat in a wine press (to avoid detection by the marauding Midianites) when the call of God came to him. "The LORD is with you, O valiant warrior" (Judges 6:12). Now either God was mocking Gideon by calling him a valiant warrior, or God's idea of a warrior is very different from ours.

What made Gideon a victor was not his background, or his life up to the point of God's call to him. It was his life *after* the call that shows his stand as a victor. He apparently was not naturally courageous; or a great leader of men. Gideon was a victor, not because of his natural abilities, but because of the attitude of his heart. He was willing to trust God *in action*.

Gideon relied on God to work through his weakness. Once he was convinced of God's call to him, he acted on that call. He destroyed the altar of Baal (at night because he was afraid of the people) and raised an army of 33,000 men to attack the Midianite army, which numbered 135,000. By the time Gideon's army was ready to attack the Midianites, God had winnowed the army down to only 300 men.

With his forces shrunk to less than a hundredth of its original strength, Gideon was cautious and wanted confirmation from God. He tested God by laying two fleeces before Him. One night the fleece was soaking wet and the ground dry, the next night the fleece was dry and the ground wet—both in confirmation of Gideon's questions about whether or not it really was God who was leading him. Even after God spoke through the fleeces, Gideon was still afraid. Because of his fear, God instructed him to sneak down to the Midianite camp and listen to what the enemy was saying. Gideon heard the fear in the enemy and attacked that night, defeating the whole Midianite army.

Gideon was a victor through the action he took in answer to God's call. Even in the face of doubt, he was willing to be the one through whom God worked. He was a thoroughly human victor, with fears and frailties like each of us—being a victim came as easily to Gideon as it does to any of us.

The Flavors of Tyranny

The ways to be a victim and the objects to which one can relate as a victim are too varied to count. However, the common denominator is *tyranny*. You may be tyrannized by your past, your future, your doctrine, the government, your spouse, your friends, your neighbors, your children, your enemies, among other things.

To the degree hurts of the past and fears of the future influence our present state, we are not in control of our lives and neither is God. We are victims. Salvation is not a one-time event but a journey that we enter day-to-day, a pilgrimage that we take, with God at our side, to forsake the ways of a victim and become a victor. Everyone—Christian and non-Christian alike—faces the circumstances of life and the harsh realities of this world that tempt us to yield to the comfort of being a victim.

Our success in this pilgrimage is determined in large measure by the map we use. With maps, there are two key issues: 1) Is the map detailed enough? and 2) Is the map oriented correctly with the territory? The best directions in the world are useless, as is the most detailed map, if you cannot locate your position on the map or how the map lines up with the territory.

The question, "who or what is in control?" acts like a compass which helps you find yourself on the map. Just as a compass is most helpful when you refer to it throughout a journey, so is this question most helpful if you continually ask it along the way to make sure your journey is on track.

Ultimately, relating as a victim is a strategy that is designed to focus all attention on yourself so that you thereby avoid reality. External circumstances—such as the one who betrayed you, your fears of the future, your lack of time, money, energy—affect your life so unjustly that you must avenge yourself in some way to prevent being abused again, or forgotten, or destroyed. Your statement to the world is "If you were in my shoes you would do the same." Victimhood is the foundation for rebellion. Imbedded in Satan's temptation of Adam and Eve is the accusation that God is unjust and selfish; that He would not provide, therefore Adam and Eve had to wrest control from God and provide for themselves.

A set of doctrines can also be used to tyrannize. The tyranny of their doctrines and traditions is what blinded the religious leaders of Jesus' time from seeing that He was the Messiah. Israel was expecting a King, someone to militarily deliver them from the rule of the Romans. They wanted revenge. Jesus pointed the way to a different and better deliverance. He gave us an example that not only works against the tyranny of the Romans, but against all tyrants in all ages. Jesus taught a deliverance from the rule of the Romans through an internal relationship of loving God (who *is* love) with all of our being, and of loving our neighbor, even our enemy, as ourselves.

God's plan of salvation for the Israelites was to deliver them from all tyranny and all victimhood, not just the political tyranny of the Romans. His answer was *metanoia*, a total change of heart and mind; a change from lusting after revenge to forgiving.

The priests and other religious leaders so hated Roman political control that they could not accept the renewal Jesus was working in the lives of those He touched. They could not see beyond their immediate needs. They could not fit Jesus into their beliefs about the Messiah and their doctrines about how God would redeem them. They coveted liberty, yet could not see it as an attitude of the heart that superseded the external conditions of their lives. When they saw that Jesus would not give them what they wanted, they envied Him His liberty and so destroyed Him.

The expectation of the coming Messiah was running high because people could read the signs of the times, just as they can read them today. But when He came, the religious leaders refused to recognize Him because He asked them to give what they were unwilling to give. He demanded a change of heart. He asked them to love; to be responsible and face the consequences of their choices, knowing God would provide. Although they desired someone to deliver them from the outward Roman oppression, the priests were unwilling to look at the tyranny they embraced in their own hearts.

When He came and showed them an even greater deliverance than the one for which they hoped—a revival of their hope and joy—they were offended at what they had to give up to have the kingdom of God. In refusing so great a deliverance, they became victim to their Savior—the provision for their salvation became their stumbling block.

The Church, society, and individuals are in much the same state today—demanding our way and willing to slander, gossip, and destroy in order to have it. There is just as great a call in the world today for renewal as there was in the synagogue prior to Jesus' birth.

Why Do Revivals Fade?

With such a call for renewal, why do we see a downward slide in the American people, in our government, and in the Church in America? Even though God has regularly brought outbursts of revival to this country as He did to Israel, the nation continues its decline with barely a pause. This downward spiral of church and country over the last one hundred years is well documented. The statistics speak for themselves. Rape, abortion, theft, and violent crime have all increased in the last century, and especially in the past thirty years.

The wise men of the Church attribute it to causes both numerous and conflicting: the elimination of the Bible and Jesus' name from the schools, the demise of the death penalty, the ascendency of the Democrats, the spread of Communism, the pervasive materialism, the rise of Secular Humanism, the dominance of men, the militancy of women, and the break-up of the family.

This conversation is a symptom of our country being out of touch with who or what is in control. When the question of who or what is in control is forgotten or ignored, the victim determines the outcome of a situation, just as victims determined the outcome in the Garden of Eden. But hope remains that the Church today has the power to kill the victim by standing as Jesus did when He brought reform to the Jewish nation. He stood for man's liberty in life and, ultimately, for man's liberty from death.

The trend of the spiritual life of our country and church is also in decline. Revivals rarely, if ever, reach the peak of what was common in past generations. Where are the Jonathan Edwards[1] of today, under whose preaching whole communities are converted? Instead, we settle for large meetings where the same set of fence sitters commit and recommit themselves through the same old altar calls.

Just before a revival takes place, its anticipated peak often seems like a radical jump upward. But that peak, although an anointed event, is still lower than those before it. Why? This, and other manifestations of a long-term decline in the spiritual life of the church, is directly linked to the increasing

---

[1]The Puritan preacher who, along with George Whitefield, started the Great Awakening in 18th Century America.

victimhood of our society. The manifestations of victimhood are pervasive today: broken marriages, inner-city anarchy, the welfare state, and fatherless families to name just a few. Our goal is to reverse this decline by attacking the root, rather than flaying the branches. Our vision is for the next revival to be more powerful, more deeply implanted into the hearts of men and women, and longer lasting than the previous one. Dare we even hope and dream of continuous revival?

Reform is not cheap. It is costly. It cost Jesus his life and will continue to cost us our comforts and conveniences, until He returns to set all things true. Reform begins with the individual and is finally appreciated socially when enough individuals have paid the price. The words of Frederick Douglass, a great orator from the Civil War era, poignantly describe the commitment required to reform an individual and a nation. In a letter written to a fellow abolitionist who was appalled by the cost being paid by the reformers, Douglass wrote:

Let me give you a word on the philosophy of reform. The whole history of the progress of human liberty shows that all concessions yet made to her august claims have been born of earnest struggle. The conflict has been exciting, agitating, all absorbing, and for the time being putting all other tumults to silence. It must do this or it does nothing. If there is no struggle there is no progress. Those who profess to favor freedom, and yet depreciate agitation, are men who want crops without plowing up the ground. They want rain without thunder and lightning. They want the ocean without the awful roar of its waters. This struggle may be a moral one, it may be a physical one, or it may be both moral and physical; but it must be a struggle. Power concedes nothing without a demand! It never did and it never will. Find out just what a people will submit to and you have found the exact amount of injustice and wrong which will be imposed upon them; and these will continue until they are resisted with either words or blows, or with both. The limits of tyrants are prescribed by the endurance of those whom they oppress.[2]

Think of a problem that keeps reoccurring in your life, over which you seem to have experienced little lasting victory. Perhaps it's outbursts of anger and rage; lustful thoughts and fantasies; unbridled fears; rancor, bitterness, and strife; ravenous envy; deep depressions and lethargy; episodes of dominating pride; riotous eating and drinking. How do you respond when confronted with it? Do you offer the victim's answer: "It is my history, my parents, the circumstances, our form of government, the party running the country, the Democratic President, and so on," and thus give up the struggle to reform your life because you have "found the answer" in blaming the outside world?

All the books you've read, seminars you've attended, and sermons you've heard have not provided a lasting victory. When was the last time you heard anyone stop and consider the impact of his own love or lack of love on the condition of his relationships, his Church, his community, or his country? How many people do you know, including yourself, who are willing to consider that their way of relating could be the root of the problems about which they complain? Who believes that the reform you seek from others must begin within?

---

[2]Letter to Gerrit Smith, March 30,1849.

Who or What is in Control? / 37

What Will the Result of the Next Revival Be?

Many people believe that God is sending a great revival to American churches. But what good will a great revival do, if those touched by it think that the revival is only for them, and only for their immediate need to hear from God, to feel His presence, to be right about His will, or whatever their personal agenda may be? What if those who are revived have a vision no bigger than themselves? What will happen to God's precious gift of revival if the recipients believe that the revival depends on an outward source rather than the heart within? How will they steward their renewed life?

The scripture says the gift of the Comforter is not just for us, but that we may in turn comfort others: "Blessed be the God and Father of our Lord Jesus Christ, the Father of mercies and God of all comfort; who comforts us in all our affliction so that we may be able to comfort those who are in any affliction with the comfort with which we ourselves are comforted by God" (II Corinthians 1:3-4). His precious gift of comfort has been dying from increasing neglect over the last seventeen hundred years. The individual, the Church, and the Nation will continue to decline as long as each generation selfishly hoards God's outpouring of revival for its own selfish purposes. Unless one generation is willing to take the responsibility that Jesus calls us to take and steward our revived lives for the glory of God and the good of others, then our communities will decline and we will once again not be able to identify Him when He comes into our midst.

Where Are All the Cathedral Builders?

In the twelfth century, a wave of building began. Ever larger and more magnificent cathedrals were built for the glory of God and the prestige of cities. The leaders who envisioned these mammoth building projects and rallied the necessary financial support and material resources rarely saw their dream completed. The average cathedral took 80 years to finish; some building projects lasted 200 years. The first generation hired an architect, who both designed and supervised the construction of the cathedral.

The cathedrals' floor plans were in the shape of a cross. Building progressed in stages. The top of the cross, or *choir*, was constructed first. Off of the choir, five to seven chapels were built like petals radiating from a daisy. The cross beam, or *transept*, was built next; finally the *nave*, or long upright of the cross was completed. Cathedral vaults reached heights of 80 to 160 feet. The spires and towers could be twice that height.

The first generation realized that they would never see the completion of their dream. They governed themselves however, by the way they lived day-to-day with their neighbors and their children, in order to see that their vision was finished by the third generation.

They told stories of the importance of the cathedral, what it meant to God and the coming generations, the prestige that it would bring to the city. They built into their children a reverence for the task, and a sense of meaning and purpose. They passed on the responsibility of the vision so thoroughly that members of the next generation committed their lives to honor the future their parents saw and to take on the vision for themselves.

Cathedral building is a metaphor for a way of living as a victor. It is driven by *cathedral thinking*. This is what Jesus was doing when He commanded us to love God with all our heart, soul, strength, and mind, and our neighbor as ourselves. He made it clear that the Father's concern was the heart of man and that the heart ought to be our concern, too, in making disciples of the nations. He knew that the only way to make disciples of the nations was through loving. No crusades, no inquisitions, no coerced conversions to favored doctrines can accomplish what a relationship of love with God and one another can accomplish. The purpose He sets before every man and woman is to be governed by love; to be responsible to another; to love as I would have another love me.

Love is the soil from which all relationships are born and responsibility the foundation upon which they are built. A victor is someone who continually inquires about who or what is in control; someone who unswervingly works within the constraints of the circumstances to have his vision become a reality.

2. Reality Will Set You Free

Jesus said to him, "I am the way, and the truth, and the life; no one comes to the Father, but through Me."

John 14:6

Reality has a wonderful quality about it—it doesn't care how you feel or what you think. It makes no bones about being brutally honest. You never need worry whether reality is coddling you with half-truths. No matter what your opinion is of any subject, reality is true to itself. Rocks are hard and water is wet. Even if you think and wish it to be different, rocks are not velvet and water is not dry. Reality is what it is.

What we *make* of reality is another matter. Between each of us and reality sits our own unique interpretations. They are our belief systems, our world views, our perceptual filters. Whatever label we place on them, our interpretations consist of our on-going conversation, conscious and unconscious, about the meaning of what we experience. Our interpretations color and direct our thoughts and our feelings. Our own individual histories, our unique experiences, and our culture add layers to the filters through which we interpret reality.

In Numbers 13, the spies that Moses sent to survey the Promised Land are a perfect example of filtering reality through subjective filters. The Lord directed Moses to send a leader from each of the tribes of Israel to spy out the land. These twelve surveyed the area for 40 days.

When they returned, the *facts* they reported were consistent: the land was fruitful, flowing with milk and honey; and the people living in the Promised Land were strong. But the conclusions the spies reached split them into two opposing camps. Caleb and Joshua wanted to go in and conquer the land; the rest argued that Israel was too weak to take the land. Hear what the second group said:

> But the men who had gone up with him [Caleb] said, "We are not able to go up against the people, for they are too strong for us." So they gave out to the sons of Israel a bad report of the land which they had spied out, saying, "The land through which we have gone, in spying it out, is a land that devours its inhabitants; and all the people whom we saw in it are men of great size. . . . [A]nd we became like grasshoppers *in our own sight*, and so we were in their sight." (Numbers 13:31-33; italics added)

God's judgment of this interpretation was dreadful—He decreed that all the people of Israel wander in the wilderness one year for each day that the spies were in the land. Everyone in that generation died before entering the Promised Land except for Joshua and Caleb.

The judgment fell upon all the people, not just their leaders. The people were not spared by the excuse that they were not directly involved in bringing back the assessment. They could have chosen to believe Joshua and Caleb, instead, they chose to believe the evil report. Their hearts were revealed when they desired to return to the bondage of Egypt because of the report of the negative majority. Look at the connection between the leaders and the people from God's perspective and you will see God's principle of community. We *do* bear responsibility for the state of our communities; we *are* our brothers' keepers.[3] What this responsibility entails we will explore later.

We must take care not to confuse reality with our *interpretation* of reality. How we see ourselves—"we became like grasshoppers in our own sight"—determines how others see us—"and so we were in their sight." Caleb and Joshua saw another reality—that God was on Israel's side and therefore Israel would prevail. Had Israel embraced this understanding of reality, how then would the giants have viewed them? Undoubtedly their faith in God and their fortitude—their willingness to die in battle—would have struck fear in their enemies' hearts.

What makes an interpretation evil rather than good is the direction in which it takes us. Does our interpretation lead us to be more steadfast in love for God and others, more thoroughly persuaded of God's purpose for us, strengthened in the hope of God's deliverance as did Joshua's and Caleb's interpretation? Then it is good. If the interpretation leads in the opposite direction, toward complacency and apathy or self-pity, it is evil.

Complacency is defined by Webster as self-satisfaction. Its main objective is to secure predictable comfort. To most of the spies, the work of conquering the inhabitants of the promised land looked overwhelming; a task which would call them to a moment-by-moment dependence on God. It was the antithesis of predictable comfort. The negative majority led the people to an interpretation of reality that matched their own

---

[3]Cain coined this phrase in Genesis 4:9. The word 'keeper' comes from the Hebrew root *shamar-* meaning "to guard, to keep watch and ward, to protect" according to Brown-Driver-Brigg's Hebrew dictionary. This comes close to the meaning of loving our neighbor as ourselves.

complacency and drove them to desire the predictability of Egyptian slavery.

By embracing a weak and helpless interpretation of reality, we enslave ourselves. This is what a victim does. But in the midst of the slavery lies a truth that becomes a lifeline. We can judge how close to reality our interpretation is by whether or not it leads us toward greater freedom and liberty, or toward greater bondage.

Truth as Reality

Knowing the truth sets us free (John 8:32), Jesus says, and truth and reality are intimately connected. In fact, the definition in both Hebrew and Greek for "truth" is "reality."[4] This similarity of meaning in both languages is lost among the many philosophical and cultural differences of Hebrew and Greek thought. The Hebrew language and culture were concrete and earthy, whereas the Greek language and culture were more esoteric and intellectual. Although one can make too much of differences in the Hebrew and Greek languages, the dichotomy points out two distinct approaches to knowledge that we can adopt.

The Hebrew mindset says to get to know someone, follow him around for a few days. Then based on the reality of what you saw, you would know him—a knowledge based on his

---

[4]For example, the Greek word for truth is *aletheia*: "Truth, reality; the unveiled reality lying at the basis of and agreeing with an appearance; the manifested, the veritable essence of matter. . . .Truth as evidenced in relation to facts, therefore, *aletheia* denotes the reality clearly lying before our eyes as opposed to a mere appearance, without reality." Spiros Zodhiates, *The Complete Word Study Dictionary: New Testament*, 120.

actions, not his words. You would see if he made and kept promises; how he related to his family, his friends, and his enemies. Was he accountable for what he said; did he hold others accountable? What were his priorities and what were not?

On the other hand, the Greek mindset is philosophical and propositional, much like our own culture's. To get to know someone, a Greek would ask her what she believed. Then based on her propositions and beliefs, the Greek would claim to know her.

A powerful example of the Hebraic world view is Deuteronomy 30, where, before they cross the Jordan, Moses charges the generation following the one that died in the wilderness:

See, I have set before you today life and prosperity, and death and adversity; in that I command you today to love the LORD your God, to walk in His ways and to keep His commandments and His statutes and His judgments, that you may live and multiply, and that the LORD your God may bless you in the land where you are entering to possess it. But if your heart turns away and you will not obey, but are drawn away and worship other gods and serve them, I declare to you today that you shall surely perish. You shall not prolong your days in the land where you are crossing the Jordan to enter and possess it. I call heaven and earth to witness against you today, that I have set before you life and death, the blessing and the curse. So choose life in order that you may live, you and your descendants, by loving the LORD your God, by obeying His voice, and by holding fast to Him; for this is your life and the length of your days, that you may live in the land which the LORD swore to your fathers, to Abraham, Isaac, and Jacob, to give them. (Deuteronomy 30:15-20)

Moses calls heaven and earth—the reality of the physical universe—to be both a witness to and against the people. Their history as a people bore witness against the Israelites that day: being miraculously called out of bondage and saved from the hand of Pharaoh's army in the parting of the Red Sea, the many miracles that God performed to supply their needs in the wilderness, the pillar of fire, and the cloud of smoke. Moses called them to reality from the perspective of God's protection and provision, rather than from fear and the desire for comfort.

Christ also calls us to reality—to observe the physical universe with eyes made alive to the Reality that He is. In the light of Christ and His work, we can live in this moment with an eye toward eternal life with Him. This eternal perspective provides us with the freedom to serve others rather than ourselves, and thus to love God by loving "the least of these." Knowing reality sets us free from bondage.

Unlike the Hebraic culture of Moses' and Jesus' day, propositional truths hold tremendous sway in our modern world. Politicians can openly profess positions that they inwardly despise and we think they are sincere. We view religious people as pure and holy or misguided and evil based on what they say their doctrine is. In business, we make deals and then cancel them when they become inconvenient, based on thin legal arguments. These examples, and countless others, are possible because of the confusion between *knowing* truths and *being* true to the truth we know.

This confusion ultimately leads to despair. The belief that knowing truths (such as knowing the chapter and verse on an issue, knowing the five variations in translation, knowing all the supporting and detracting arguments) is the same as living the reality that the text describes, is called *textualism*.[5] When we recognize no distinction between textualism and actually *living* the truth that we believe, we lose hope. We act as if we are true to all the truths we know, when—in reality—we know we are not. Textualism runs deep in the evangelical church in America.

From a non-Christian's first introduction to salvation in a step-by-step pamphlet, to sitting in a pew and raising a hand

---

[5]Jesus spoke to this issue in His Sermon on the Mount:

"Beware of the false prophets, who come to you in sheep's clothing, but inwardly are ravenous wolves. You will know them by their fruits. Grapes are not gathered from thorn bushes, nor figs from thistles, are they? Even so, every good tree bears good fruit; but the bad tree bears bad fruit. A good tree cannot produce bad fruit, nor can a bad tree produce good fruit. Every tree that does not bear good fruit is cut down and thrown into the fire. So then, you will know them by their fruits. Not everyone who says to Me, 'Lord, Lord,' will enter the kingdom of heaven; but he who does the will of My Father who is in heaven. Many will say to Me on that day, 'Lord, Lord, did we not prophesy in Your name, and in Your name cast out demons, and in Your name perform many miracles?' And then I will declare to them, 'I never knew you; depart from Me, you who practice lawlessness'" (Matthew 7:15-23).

The criterion for Jesus' approval is that of relationship. The first characteristic of the fruit is that it is physical and real. The second characteristic of the fruit is that it comes out of a genuine relationship with Jesus and an alignment with the Father's will. Just using Jesus' name to cast out demons, to heal, and to perform many miracles is not sufficient evidence of this genuine relationship. Physical fruit is necessary. A tree by its nature produces fruit; Jesus treated fruitless trees harshly. See the fig tree mentioned in Matthew 21 and Mark 11.

with every head bowed and every eye closed, to the approach and content of new believers' classes, the emphasis in many churches is on learning "truth." Then, based on the propositional truth that the truth shall set you free, freedom is declared, regardless of the reality of the person's life.

The result is a church body in which few if any members will speak honestly about their hurts and failures. When someone courageously exposes their shortcomings, all too often they receive judgment rather than mercy.

Believers are left in confusion and despair with little hope of reconciling the dichotomy between doctrine and practice. This confusion and despair is a major cause of disillusionment and lethargy in the church. The dichotomy between doctrine and practice was shown to be illusory when Jesus said that "everyone who looks on a woman to lust for her has committed adultery with her already in his heart" (Matthew 5:28). Jesus destroyed the belief that we can keep our internal stance of heart disconnected from our actions. Whatever is in our heart will shine through our actions.

Textualism has eternal consequences: on the Day of Judgement, we will be accounting for our *actions*. Pointing to our intentions will not justify us on that day, because our intentions *always* work themselves out as actions. The proof of the intention is in the action. The Judge of our souls cares little for intentions that are never birthed into action.

Textualism makes the error of confusing the means with the end. Knowing truths is the first step to being true to them.

Anyone can claim to be an Alpine skier while standing in the starting gate. An imposter could answer many questions about Alpine racing: the best skis, the best wax, how to take the best line through a curve and so on. She may *know* the best techniques, the best times, the best skiers. In the starting gate, however, her claim is untested. Her claim can even appear true as she takes the first few yards of the slalom course. But the true Alpine skier is known by whether or not she finishes the race. In like manner, the end for every Christian is not just to *know* he or she is saved and redeemed; but to *live* a life that is saved and redeemed.

As John the Apostle wrote, "Little children, let us not love with word or with tongue, but in deed and truth" (I John 3:18). The deeds of love speak clearly the words and intentions that go before them.

Freedom for What?

If truth is not the end objective, it follows that neither is freedom an end in itself. What is the point of being set free? In a physical sense, we are all uncomfortably free to do whatever we please; and as Christians, we are set free spiritually as well. But that is not enough. Think of Jesus. He was physically and spiritually free. He never missed the mark by sinning. But living in spiritual and physical freedom, even though it is a blessing, was not Jesus' mission on earth. It was necessary, however, and essential for His mission as the Lamb of God. For Jesus and for us as well, spiritual freedom is not the end, it is the starting place.

The purpose of being free is to establish our unique vision as a reality. Although the major distinguishing difference between victims and victors is that the first are governed by circumstances and the latter by vision, circumstances and vision are not opposed. Circumstances never have to shift to create the space for vision. Vision exists in, around, and throughout the circumstances. Believing that the circumstances have to change or disappear for a vision to become a reality is a victim's rationalization. The commitment behind a vision will stop at nothing to establish itself in reality. In fact, in the circumstances themselves, vision will see God's provision. Rather than a stop, the circumstances become the fuel for transformation.

The difference between a vision that sees God's provision in the circumstances and a 'vision' that appears similar but is still a 'victim's vision' is seen in the visions of Jesus and Judas. Externally at least, their visions appeared the same—that of establishing the kingdom of God on earth in Israel. The path each chose to attain the vision, however, was very different. Jesus chose to suffer death on the cross in order to deliver into God's hands a Church without spot or wrinkle. It seems for Judas, on the other hand, that the Kingdom was almost entirely *of this world*. He handled the money, cared little for the poor, and, as a Zealot, thought the best way to achieve the kingdom of God on earth was to cut back-room deals in order to force Jesus' hand.

Judas suffered from the supremely human flaw of thinking that everyone, even Jesus, was like him. He put himself in Jesus' place and thought that if he were to choose between dying or establishing himself as king in all the earth, he would choose the latter. The basis of his thinking and acting was selfishness. His decision revealed the basis of his vision.

Judas's two errors—trying to manipulate God and others to do what he wanted and presuming that God and others are like him in every way—are deeply embedded in the human heart and thus in the church. How often do we relate to our loved ones in ways to get them to behave according to our wishes? How often do pastors and parishioners maneuver each other so that the other "toes the line"? These errors cover up the deep insecurity we experience because the future is uncertain.

A desire to manipulate and control often arises in situations of great stress and threat. This was true for Judas. The cross did not figure into his equation. The cross threatened his position as one of the twelve disciples. He planned to judge the tribes of Israel; his vision was of a throne, not of Jesus' death.[6] His vision was oriented to and grounded in the four principles of selfishness: looking good, feeling good, being right, and being in control.

Jesus' vision, in complete opposition to Judas's, looked toward others and contributing to their visions. Not only was His vision directed toward serving others, it was generative—the impact He made on people spread to others. His sacrifice opened up possibilities for others and is the hallmark of loving His neighbor as Himself.

How many people, rather than being set free by the truth they know and profess, are tyrannized by that very truth, and in turn tyrannize others? In contrast, *being* true benefits others in specific, tangible ways. If we have the truth, and yet are not set free, the only conclusion is that we are holding the truth for ourselves, rather than for the benefit of others.

Jesus sets each of us free in order to join Him in His work—willing the good of others. Vision calls us into action. The vision is then funneled into a prudent plan of action contained in a set of promises. These are spelled out with conditions and a timeframe for fulfillment. How we translate our vision into promises shows the commitment with which we made the promises.

With promises and commitments made, responsibility and accountability come into play. As a whole, promises and

---

[6]See Luke 22:28-30: "And you are those who have stood by Me in My trials; and just as My Father has granted Me a kingdom, I grant you that you may eat and drink at My table in My kingdom, and you will sit on thrones judging the twelve tribes of Israel."

commitments, responsibility and accountability form the structure within which prudent action can occur. In this sense, *prudent* means "effective for bringing about the fulfillment of a promise within the bounds of the other virtues of the Christian life."[7]

With a structure of fulfillment in place, we can produce a rich harvest. An other-centered community will develop with Jehovah-Jireh, God the Provider, as the center.

Rich harvests require that the grain be sifted. For example, in sifting wheat, the grains of wheat are first ground between stones to crack the outer cover of the kernel. Then the grain is separated from the chaff by tossing it in the air, where the wind blows away the lighter chaff. In our relationships with each other, accountability and responsibility represent the sifting process.

Sifting is a refining process which brings pain and suffering and every kind of attack to frustrate us from pursuing our vision. How we respond to the attack defines whether the sifting is good news or bad news. When our focus is on serving the other, the sifting is good news because it burns out any selfishness that corrupts the purity of our vision, promise, and commitment. Peter was more effective in serving others after the sifting of his betrayal at the crucifixion, followed by his restoration after the resurrection.

The energy to endure the trials and tribulations inherent with declaring a vision are embedded in the vision itself. Is the vision of a future worth having big enough to overcome the pain of falling short, being sifted, and going again? Is it worth

----

[7]The 13th-century theologian Thomas Aquinas identified a total of seven Christian virtues: love, hope, faith, prudence, temperance, fortitude, and justice.

the discomfort, disturbance, and turbulence caused in the wake of pursuing a promise with iron-clad commitment?

Whenever we pursue a vision wholeheartedly, the areas of our lives in which we struggle with being a victim begin to surface. The roadblocks we encounter will be exactly those areas in which we relate irresponsibly.

When I (Dan) was about 12 years old, my dad and I would visit my grandfather on the weekends. One weekend Grandpa asked me if I wanted to work. I said, "Yes! I'd love to work." He told me he would pay me to keep his yard green.

After two weeks of faithfully working on my grandfather's yard, I approached him to be paid. He went out on the lawn and came back in a lather. "Why Danny," he said, "you haven't done your job. How can you expect me to pay you?"

I left in tears, completely humiliated and bewildered. What had I done? I'd put in so many hours on the lawn. I thought grandfather would be pleased.

When I told my father what had happened. He called grandpa and came away from the phone equally perturbed: "Son," he said, "you're killing grandpa's grass by over fertilizing it! He's paying you for a green yard, not for working hard! You're confused about what your job is."

My grandfather's request was specific, as was my promise —to make the yard green. But the physical universe revealed the posture of my heart. I was actually more interested in making money and gaining my grandfather's approval, than in meeting his need or keeping my promise. The brown grass testified eloquently to that! Nor would working harder have made any difference if I continued to do the same things.

I raged against my father and my grandfather when they pointed out my obvious selfishness. The more I sulked in my humiliation and shame, the more they refused to play into my need for self-significance. I turned to my mother for sympathy. I threw a tantrum and tried to get her to force them to be "nice" to me (code for getting my own way). I did everything I could to hide from looking at my own selfishness. I was furious that nothing worked. Finally, I figured out that what I needed to do was to get my grandfather's grass to grow! It was that simple and that complex.

3. The Humiliation of the Cross

If anyone wishes to come after Me, let him deny himself, and take up his cross, and follow Me. For whoever wishes to save his life shall lose it; but whoever loses his life for My sake shall find it.

Matthew 15:24-25

Life is humiliating. Every humiliation comes to us in answer to our own arrogance—the arrogance of the master, or actually the arrogance of the one *trying* to be the master. The experience of humiliation is that of being lowered from the position that we think we deserve to one that we *know* that we don't. Jesus' parable of the dinner guests speaks to this:

And He began speaking a parable to the invited guests when He noticed how they had been picking out the places of honor at the table; saying to them, "When you are invited by someone to a wedding feast, do not take the place of honor, lest someone more distinguished than you may have been invited by him, and he who invited you both shall come and say to you, 'Give place to this man,' and then in disgrace you proceed to occupy the last place. But when you are invited, go and recline at the last place, so that when the one who has invited you comes, he may say to you, 'Friend, move up higher'; then you will have honor in the sight of all who are at the table with you. For everyone who exalts himself shall be humbled, and he who humbles himself shall be exalted." (Luke 14:7-11)

Depending on which direction you are coming from, the seat you end up in will either be the provision of God or a disgrace. The seat itself doesn't change! The difference is in the attitude of heart.

The frequency with which life humiliates us, however different the particulars, corresponds with our attempts to be master—the urge in us to be God. By being subject to the human limitations of space and time, the urge in each of us to be omnipotent and omnipresent, which is the manifestation of our basic urge to be God, is frustrated and humiliated.

As babies, our sense of omnipotence is complete. As "king baby," we wailed a summons and someone appeared. We threw a cup on the floor and someone fetched it. We squawked and someone picked us up. We commanded the universe. This sense of omnipotence was matched exactly by our helplessness and lack of power; however, we were unaware of it. Only in becoming self-aware does a baby come to know the humiliation of being human. He begins to find that his command of the universe is an illusion and rails against it.

I (Derek) remember my son walking with me into a toy store when he was two years old. As we passed a huge stuffed teddy bear, he pointed and declared in an imperious voice, "Mine!" I did not buy him the bear and he screamed all the way home. The last thing he wanted was to accept either his own physical limitations or the limits I imposed upon him. Yet, developing as a person involves the growing awareness and acceptance of the limitations of being human—becoming aware of what we *can* influence and control, and more importantly, knowing those areas over which we have no power. Each lesson we learn frustrates and humiliates us in our desire to be God. In order to come to maturity, we suffer humiliation upon humiliation. Even Jesus, the Son of God, learned obedience and maturity through suffering (Hebrews 5:8). He, too, experienced the powerlessness and humiliation of childhood. We presume from the Biblical record, that He lost his earthly father Joseph at an early age. To what we don't know but we do know He was a man of sorrows and acquainted with grief (Isaiah 53:3) and yet He never became a victim. Being the oldest son, the burden of caring for His mother and brothers and sisters fell upon His slender shoulders. In the rough and tumble border town of Nazareth, He surely witnessed the cruelty of man's inhumanity to man—the brutality of the occupying military, the prostitutes following after the Roman soldiers, and so on. Surely Jesus suffered taunting, if nothing else, at the hands of the older boys of the town—after all, wasn't He born three months early? What about that mother of His anyway? Her morals were proven to be suspect.

The easiest way to shrug off life's humiliations is to become a victim through blame shifting! Humiliation, rather than teaching us our limitations and therefore a dependence on God as Provider, can become a springboard to being self-righteous and self-sufficient, even superior. We say things like: "Can you believe what happened to me?" Or, "This is grossly unfair. If it weren't for my inept boss, I'd be the vice president of sales by now." Or, "My marriage would work if my wife/husband would love me more."

In our work with the *Momentus* trainings, we at Mashiyach often see the power of victimhood used to justify feelings of superiority. In one training, a participant stood up and began pacing the room. Finally, he broke down crying and complained, "Nobody here has experienced the pain that I have. None of you can understand how paralyzing the fear of further pain and rejection is for me. How difficult it is for me to relate and take the initiative with my wife and others." He went on and on in this vein, asserting his right to his superiority based on the amount of pain he had endured. The pain, rather than humbling him, had allowed him to justify the state of his failed marriage. As his self-serving diatribe was winding down, a woman quietly stood up. When he was finished, she pulled up the sleeve of her blouse and approached him. She silently held up her arm and revealed the identification number of a Nazi concentration camp. The woman then said, "Don't tell me about how much pain you've been through. I was in a concentration camp from the age of three until the age of nine. All my family died there, except me. There have been many times I wanted to die from *my* pain—but the pain reminds me that I am *alive*. Many others would gladly have traded dying in the camps for a life of pain. How long will you allow the pain of your past to define how you live in the moment?"

The room was silent as there was nothing left to say.

Experiencing the Cross

Humiliation is the mainstay of God's plan for our maturing. It is the experience of the cross. Without humiliation, our selfish heart is never pierced, we never experience compunction, one of the lost disciplines of the Church. Allan Jones describes compunction or *penthos* as "a kind of 'puncturing' of the heart. *Penthos* . . . is the word for that which pierces us to the heart, cuts us to the quick, raises us from the 'dead.' "[8]

Compunction allows our hearts to feel the injustices of our lives and the lives of others. Without the cross to bring

---

[8]Alan Jones, *Soul Making*, 84.

compunction, the victim in each of us thrives on using the injustices of life to justify all manner of selfishness: the unwillingness to love, the numbing of our feelings for others, abusive anger, or the satisfaction of numerous lusts.

Life treats each of us unjustly—people treat us with indifference, accidents happen to us and our loved ones, our well laid plans come to naught and so forth. The list is endless. And each injustice gives us an opportunity to build character. We can either endure life's injustices with as much grace and faith we can muster, or we can rail against them and use them as a license to abuse others.

I (Derek) know a man, Greg, who had been treated unjustly in several business ventures as a young man. In each instance, Greg had played a vital role in the success of the business, but had been cut out of the resulting financial rewards. Some years later, he started another business with several acquaintances. This time, Greg was determined to be in control of the situation. He took advantage of his position to cheat others in the same way others had cheated him. Of course, Greg didn't view his *own* actions as unjust—he justified them by claiming that his junior co-owners "needed to pay their dues." The "dues" he thought his partners needed to pay were the very ones he had suffered in earlier ventures. His prior hurts became his excuse to take more than his share of the benefits of the business.

This man, like so many others, chose the easy way that he knew and refused to do the hard work to end the cycle of abuse. The Bible calls this work "taking up your cross." Jesus' understanding of the cross is powerfully revealed in Matthew 16:13-26. The passage opens with Jesus asking the disciples who the people thought He was. Peter enthusiastically jumped in with "Thou art the Christ, the Son of the living God." Jesus blesses Peter for this revelation from heaven; then He goes on to show His disciples that He must go to Jerusalem to die and be raised on the third day.

In verse 22, Peter, who just moments before had shown such marvelous insight, falls dramatically and takes Jesus aside to discuss this disturbing revelation of His coming death and resurrection.

> And Peter took Him aside and began to rebuke Him, saying, "God forbid it, Lord! This shall never happen to You."

Then Jesus turns to Peter and publicly rebukes and humiliates him:

> But He turned and said to Peter, "Get behind me Satan! You are a stumbling block to me; for you are not setting your mind on God's interests, but man's. Then Jesus turned to the disciples and said, "If anyone wishes to come after Me, let him deny himself, and *take up his cross*, and follow Me. For whoever wishes to save his life shall lose it; but whoever loses his life for My sake shall find it. For what will a man be profited, if he gains the whole world, and forfeits his soul? Or what will a man give in exchange for his soul? (Matthew 16:24-26, italics added)

These are hard sayings from start to finish—not only the Lord's rebuke of Peter, but his exhortation to all of his disciples to take up their cross and follow him. Let us remember that He stated this before His own crucifixion and that crucifixion as a form of execution was well understood in the Roman world as a horrific, humiliating death; something to be avoided, not pursued. Furthermore, He speaks in paradoxes—whoever saves his life must lose it, etc. What does this all mean?

What then *does* it mean to take up your cross? How does the experience show up in your life or another's life? How do you *know* that you *have* taken up your cross? Part of the difficulty in interpreting this passage is understanding what Jesus meant by the metaphor of the cross. Understanding this metaphor is the key to living as a Christian.

We commonly understand this metaphor to mean to put down all fleshly desires and thoughts so that we can then freely love our neighbor. However, this understanding contributes to the very problem it is trying to solve. While we are certainly to mortify the sinful deeds of the flesh, one of the more subtle ploys of the enemy (or of *our* willfully deluded selves!) is to get us so caught in introspection and dealing with the self that we forget others. We miss the opportunity of being with our neighbor and loving him. We then also have a convenient excuse to focus on ourselves rather than on our neighbors. While Jesus hung on the cross, His heart and His focus remained on his neighbor. In the midst of his pain, He declared His forgiveness toward not only His tormentors, but all of us.

Spiros Zodhiates, a Greek scholar and author of *The Complete Word Study Dictionary: New Testament*, makes the following comment under the entry for *stauros,* which is the Greek word for cross.

> When we read of the antagonism to the cross of Christ, we must understand it as antagonism to a redemption which was accomplished by the deepest humiliation, not by the display of power and glory . . . . The cross of Christ represents His death as suffering and connects it with the curse of sin. The cross shows this peculiar manner of His

death as that which entailed *suffering shame, rejection, and humiliation.*[9]

In asking us to take up our cross, could Jesus really be asking us to choose the suffering of shame, rejection, and humiliation? This is as unpopular an idea today, as it was in Isaiah's time, when he wrote, "Behold, I have refined you, but not as silver; I have tested you in the furnace of affliction" (Isaiah 48:10). There are lone voices crying out that God never promised us a trouble-free life.[10] But these seem the exception rather than the rule.

Shame, Rejection, and Humiliation

Based on the meaning of the phrase as Jesus used it, taking up our cross has *everything* to do with taking on the suffering of shame, rejection, and humiliation. In contrast, popular, tabloid psychology says these are experiences to avoid. Shame, particularly that breed of shame known as "toxic shame," is damaging to the psyche. Rejection causes life-long scars and should certainly be avoided. In my experiences as a *Momentus* trainer, I have seen that fear of rejection is one of the primary reasons that people remain stuck in mediocre and often painful relationships. Fear of being rejected prevents them from

---

[9] Spiros Zodhiates, *The Complete Word Study Dictionary: New Testament*, 1308-1309, italics added.

[10] One lone voice is Dr. Larry Crabb in his book, *Inside Out.* In secular society moreover, psychologists such as Carl Jung often define neurosis as the avoidance of *necessary* suffering.

changing the status quo and risking themselves in order to touch another.

The first two verses of Hebrews 12 tell us how Jesus responded to humiliation, shame, and rejection:

> let us run with endurance the race that is set before us, fixing our eyes on Jesus, the author and perfecter of faith, who for the joy set before Him endured the cross, *despising the shame*, and has sat down at the right hand of the throne of God [italics added].

The word translated here as "despising" means "to think little or nothing of." There was no more disgraceful way to die than by crucifixion, yet Jesus counted the shame of the Cross as little or nothing.

In contrast, we regard shame, rejection, and humiliation as ruinous. We are amazed that anyone would willfully suffer disgrace. Furthermore, to urge someone to think little of it invites the accusation that we want people to 'stuff their feelings' and deny reality.

The reality is that Jesus did feel shame, rejection, and humiliation. He felt it more deeply and completely than we ever shall. But even feeling as deeply as He did, the *relationship* He took to those feelings was one of thinking little of them. He chose to disregard them. He scoffed at them. He refused to be a victim to his feelings; they weren't an excuse for his breaking his word.

How different from our first response! We desire to feel important by making our difficulties significant. We explode the smallest twinge of humiliation into an earth-shattering event in order to comfort and justify ourselves. But by making big the humiliations we suffer, we end up hobbling ourselves. By making them bigger than they are, we increase our desire to avoid them. No wonder we turn away any time we might experience shame, humiliation, or rejection. We run from the slightest whiff of any of these as from a deadly poison.

Jesus demonstrates that determining how "big" or "small" a humiliation is depends on us. He compared the shame to the joy set before Him. In that comparison the shame meant nothing but was worth enduring in order to attain the joy. Jesus' vision of what God had promised was big enough and attractive enough to draw Him through the pain of the cross (Hebrews 12:2).

So, the next question is "how do we take up our cross?" Jesus said:

> And he who does not take his cross and follow after Me is not worthy of Me. He who has found his life shall lose it, and he who has lost his life for My sake shall find it. He who receives you receives Me, and he who receives Me receives Him who sent Me. He who receives a prophet in the name of a prophet shall receive a prophet's reward; and he who receives a righteous man in the name of a righteous man shall receive a righteous man's reward. And whoever in the name of a disciple gives to one of these little ones even a cup of cold water to drink, truly I say to you he shall not lose his reward. (Matthew 10:38-42)

Jesus reveals that it is not just *what* we are doing that is important. What we are doing does not determine whether we are worthy of Him. What makes us worthy is *in whose name* we are doing it. The Scriptures say, "whatever you do in word or deed, do all in the name of the Lord Jesus" (Colossians 3:17), and Jesus said "to the extent that you did it to one of these brothers of Mine, even the least of them, you did it to Me." (Matthew 25:40).

In whose name we minister reveals whose will we are following. Are we following our own will for our own agenda and our own reward? Or are we putting our neighbor's interest ahead of our own? The cross that Jesus asks us to bear involves considering others as more important than ourselves. Jesus said, "For whoever wishes to save his life shall lose it; but whoever loses his life for My sake and the gospel's shall save it" (Mark 8:35). If we are seeking to save ourselves, we not only lose ourselves but we become victims. In contrast, if we take up our cross and give ourselves to others through our promises as Christ did, knowing that, no matter what hurt we may encounter, the Father's hand will deliver us, we shall save our lives. This preference for the Father's will and dependence on His deliverance is what it means to lose our lives for His sake.

In whose name we are acting is the ultimate test of whether we are bearing our cross. To bear our cross is to embrace the humiliation and rejection before us, knowing that greater is Christ who lives in us than that which is in the world.

Stewards of God's Creation

For Christians, part of the humiliation of life includes realizing that we are, at most, stewards of God's creation: every possession, every asset, all the traits and gifts each of us has, is not ours, but His. We have been given them to steward. We have power over our possessions and our gifts, over our very lives to do whatever we want. Our stewardship is absolute. The parable of the talents in Eugene Peterson's paraphrase of the New Testament reads:

It's also like a man going off on an extended trip. He called his servants together and delegated responsibilities. To one he gave five thousand dollars, to another two thousand, to a third one thousand, depending on their abilities. Then he left. Right off, the first servant went to work and doubled his master's investment. The second did the same. But the man with the single thousand dug a hole and carefully buried his master's money.

After a long absence, the master of those three servants came back and settled up with them. The one given five thousand dollars showed him how he had doubled his investment. His master commended him: 'Good work! You did your job well. From now on be my partner.'

The servant with the two thousand showed how he also had doubled his master's investment. His master commended him: 'Good work! You did your job well. From now on be my partner.'

The servant given one thousand said, 'Master, I know you have high standards and hate careless ways, that you demand the best and make no allowances for error. I was afraid I might disappoint you, so I found a good hiding place and secured your money. Here it is, safe and sound down to the last cent.'

The master was furious. 'That's a terrible way to live! It's criminal to live cautiously like that! If you knew I was after the best, why did you do less than the least? The least you could have done would have been to invest the sum with the bankers, where at least I would have gotten a little interest.

Take the thousand and give it to the one who risked the most. And get rid of this "play-it-safe" who won't go out on and limb. Throw him out into utter darkness.[11]

The "play-it-safe" was afraid to risk the humiliation of the cross. He feared the impact of the wrath of the master and so avoided the possibility of a misstep by burying the talent. However the master's standard was different. The master *wanted* the servant to take risks—he was more interested in the fruit of the risk taking than the original talents he had given each one. We, too, often treat God as the "play-it-safe" treated his master. We fear that God is an evil master and act to protect ourselves from Him. We think that we need to protect the talents He has given us, rather than sowing them toward our vision of the future. In this self-protection, we miss the harvest that he intends for us to produce. God is calling us to put ourselves at stake for another through our pursuit of the vision He has set in our hearts.

For each of us, as for all stewards, a time is coming when an account will be made to the Owner of creation, the Creator Himself. Our account will be measured by a simple standard: My will or God's will.

In my (Dan's) years as a drug addict, my closest and dearest friend was a man named Carl. Carl had been a user and dealer from the time he was about 11 years old. After I finally had cleaned up my own drug addiction, my wife and I committed ourselves to help him to stop using drugs. Carl had three children, one from his first wife and two born out of wedlock. He had been divorced once and was living with his oldest son. He was dealing cocaine to make a living. His son was raising himself and often spent the night on the streets

---

[11]Eugene Peterson, *The Message*, 62-63.

because Carl locked the door during his binges and would not let anybody in—either out of paranoia about somebody killing him or because he was in a drug-induced oblivion.

Over and over, we attempted to intervene in his life, but we could not get his attention. I even went to his family to arrange an intervention, but they refused because they did not believe it would make a difference—they had given up because Carl had convinced them that he wanted to do the drugs more than he wanted them. His family told me that they did not want to risk losing what little connection they still had with him.

On one occasion Aileen and I asked him what he wanted for his three children, in order to have him focus on the prices others were paying to be in relationship with him. Carl raged at us—how could we understand? He was doing the only thing he knew how to do. He had never learned any trade other than selling drugs. I asked him to consider selling something legitimate. He said he couldn't learn new things because his father always put him down and told him he was no good. When I begged him to try for the sake of his children, he excused himself, claiming that his kids had it better than he did—at least he didn't tell them they were no good.

We debated, cajoled, pleaded, and argued with Carl late into the night. No matter what we hit him with, he came back with a victim story to justify his "death-style." We continued to pursue him for the following two years, until Carl finally died of an overdose. Even in death, his self-deception continued to live on in rumors that he was a victim: either he had been set up by dealers and given an overdose of cocaine and heroin, or he had been beaten by police. In working through the tragedy of his death with Carl's family and friends, we found almost no one who believed that all that had happened was the result of Carl's determination to follow his own will. Being a victim always gives us license, in the midst of pursuing our own selfish ends, to be right—dead right.

The tragedy of his death marred our lives. I still grieve for him, his family, and other lost young men and women, who have been hurt by betrayal and cling to that as a reason to follow their own will. By giving in to the victim inside, people like Carl give themselves license to destroy not only their lives, but to victimize those who love them deeply. In this way, Carl reenacted the same way of relating to his wife, children, and friends that his father had taken with him. Through his continued acts of selfishness, he demonstrated that his life with us was not worth living; that in his eyes, negating the pain he felt from his relationship with his father, both in being a drug addict and, eventually in dying, was more important to him than living with us.

Being a victim so often leads to victimizing others. Whatever we use to justify our license as a victim becomes the bludgeon we use to victimize others around us.

Jesus faced the same humiliations of being human that we all face. His existence was not charmed by being the Son of God. If anything, His life was even more humiliating than most of what we face. Even His birth in the stable, far exceeds the degradation of the humblest home birth. W. Phillip Keller described the lowly circumstances of birth in a stable based on an experience he had in the desert of Pakistan:

> I was in a remote village, alone, when suddenly a fierce, unexpected cloudburst and electrical storm drove me to seek shelter in a tiny mud-walled hovel. A very aged, white-bearded old man had beckoned me to come in out of the lashing fury of the storm.
>
> Bending over deeply to crawl through the low doorway, I fumbled my way into a dark and gloomy one-roomed abode. It took my eyes several minutes to adjust to the

darkness within. The place was full of acrid smoke from a small dung fire burning between three cooking stones on the earthen floor. The air was fetid with the vile odors of livestock and sheep dung, for several of these animals shared the same tiny space.

In one corner, close by the fire, crouched the frail little form of a tiny, teenage girl, possibly the old man's daughter. Her large, luminous dark eyes were filled with a certain foreboding as she clutched a tender, newborn infant to her breasts. The baby whimpered slightly as the girl, wrapped about only with a soiled, threadbare, cotton cloak, rocked it gently in her thin arms.

Not knowing any Pakistani, all I could do was huddle quietly, close to the smoky dung fire, while the storm beat upon the mud walls. Tiny rivulets of water ran down the dark walls where the rain leaked through the shabby roof.

Amid the gloom; amid the awful pungency of sheep, goat and other animal manure; amid the appalling poverty of this poor peasant's surroundings, God's Spirit spoke to me in unmistakable, unforgettable terms: *"THIS is how I came amongst men!"*[12]

I wept when I read those words to think of the utter humiliation and degradation to which our Lord descended to come among us. Yet in not one of the "humbling" circumstances of His life did Jesus miss the mark—He never once looked up at His Father and said, "This is too hard, Father! I never knew it would be like *this*, I want *out!*" He always chose God's will over His own. In every humiliation, He overcame the temptation to play the victim. In like

---

[12]W. Phillip Keller, *A Layman Looks at the Lamb of God*, 9-10.

manner, He challenges us to be like Him—to take up our cross daily and follow Him.

The account we give to God will involve whether or not we shouldered our cross daily; and if we followed Him by choosing the Father's will in each situation—in short, how we faced the humiliations of life. The testing of our mettle comes not in the best of times, but when the greatest tragedies and setbacks befall us. In these times of crisis and testing, the attitude of our hearts is revealed. God's concern is always the stance of the heart: how we relate to Him, to others, to the circumstances, and to ourselves when the chips are down. How we respond or react in times of sorrow and failure tell the true story of whom we love and serve.

Refining Character

To put it another way, life's humiliations test and refine our character. When we are faced with life's inevitable indignities are we filled with peace, walking in God's grace, fully persuaded that God is able to redeem even the greatest humiliation? A perfect example of a man trusting God to redeem him is Abraham. Indeed, Abraham's life foreshadows Jesus' charge to deny ourselves and take up our cross.

When God called Abraham to sacrifice Isaac, the son through whom the promise of God would be fulfilled, Abraham set off. Without the kind of soul-searching, reflection, and questioning in which a 20th-century Christian would engage before taking action, Abraham journeyed with Isaac and several servants to make his sacrifice to God on Mount Moriah. The trip took three days. It was *in* the journey, not before, that Abraham struggled with what God was calling him to do—to lay his cherished son whom he loved on the altar as a burnt offering to God.

During the three-day journey did Abraham observe the life and vitality of his son? Were there recriminations in Abraham against God? Did he silently question and rail against God? "How could you play with me? You taunt me by promising me a son. Then you wait until I am old to fulfill the promise. And now you take the promise away. This cannot be the God I believed in. When did you become so arbitrary and capricious?" Did he perhaps wonder if some awful sin, committed unwittingly, stood between him and his God?

After the storm of doubt and recrimination passed, did Abraham give up in despair, thinking all was lost? Did he come to believe that the dream of his descendants and heirs as plentiful as the stars in the sky and the sand of the seashore was only a fantasy?

Did he envision returning to the camp without Isaac? Did he contemplate the humiliation of being the one to destroy the promise of God? How would he face Sarah? What would he say? What *could* he say? What of the other people? The other nations? What would they think when they heard that Abraham, whom God had blessed, had destroyed the one through whom the blessing would come? Not only that, but had sacrificed him as the heathen Malachites who regularly sacrificed young boys to appease their pagan gods? The crowning humiliation would be Abraham's claim that God had told him to do it.

In spite of all that must have been going through Abraham's mind, he plodded on. Those three days must have seemed an eternity to Abraham. Each step bringing him closer to a humiliation so great, so permanent, that he might as well have been killing himself.

Regardless of the struggle, Abraham persevered; he set his face toward Mount Moriah, which in Hebrew means 'Jehovah provides.' At the base of the mountain, he told the servants to wait. Here too, did Abraham pause and ask himself, "What will the servants think when I return without Isaac? They'll think I'm mad! They'll draw back in fear and horror." As Isaac and he reached the appointed place, what happened there?

Picture a flat area on the top of Mount Moriah with two men building an altar of the stones they find lying around. One man is old, over 100 years of age. The other is young, strong, and at the threshold of manhood. For every stone that Abraham placed on the altar, Isaac must have stacked three. Isaac's strength and vitality were like that of a spring day, full of potential and hope.

What words passed between them? We do know that Isaac asked "Where is the lamb for the burnt offering?" Abraham replied, "God will provide for Himself the lamb for the burnt offering" (Genesis 22:7-8). Imagine the struggle Abraham went through to say those words. What thoughts raced through his head? When all was said and done, we know that Isaac submitted to his father—certainly he could have easily overpowered the old man—just as Jesus centuries later could have renounced the cross to save His own life, but chose instead to submit to His heavenly Father.

Now the younger man stands still for his father to bind him, then lies down dutifully on the altar, without a struggle. What must have been in Isaac's heart that he willingly submitted to Abraham? As Abraham raises the knife high over Isaac's breast, the word from God comes, "Abraham, Abraham! Do not stretch out your hand against the lad, and do nothing to him: for now I know that you fear God, since you have not withheld your son, your only son, from me" (Genesis 22:11-12). Abraham followed God's instructions all the way to the end. *Then* he saw the ram caught in the thicket. God's provision for the sacrifice!

Abraham and Isaac were willing to risk whatever was most important to them because they were fully persuaded that God had promised them victory. They were willing to take action and suffer looking like fools for God's sake, without being a victim to circumstances, God, or another.

Why God chose this path for Abraham and Isaac is a mystery—as mysterious as the paths any of us are called to walk. But in Abraham and Isaac, we have an example of being responsible. The word "responsible" is derived from a Latin root, *respondere*, meaning "to promise back." Isaac was the son of God's promise to Abraham. Abraham and Isaac's promise back to God was to trust and believe that with Him all things are possible, and to demonstrate their trust and faith through action. In standing in their promise to God regardless of the circumstances, they opened up the possibility for all of us to become children of promise (Galatians 4:28).

Every time we make a promise, we enter the same path that Abraham and Isaac walked. We face the same doubts and questions. We face the same humiliations. Promise is at the heart of the cross and, as we shall see in the next chapter, is the express nature of God. Promise is the altar upon which we lay the sacrifice of all that matters to us. As victors, full of faith and fully persuaded that with God all things are possible, we receive back the benefits of God's promises.

4. Promise—The Key to Community

A new command I give you: Love one another as I have loved you, so you must love one another.

John 13:34

Jesus told this "new" command to the eleven disciples in the Upper Room after Judas left to arrange His betrayal. How is this command new? It certainly has the flavor of "love thy neighbor as thyself," which Jesus had proclaimed much earlier in His ministry. The qualitatively new addition is that we are to love one another *as Jesus has loved us*. How, then, has Jesus loved us? Indeed, how does anyone love us?

The only tangible evidence of Jesus' love for the disciples is that He kept the promises He made to them; not only the explicit promises made in the course of being in community with them for three years, but also the implicit promises made by the Old Testament prophets regarding the Messiah. He kept them, even when he knew the coming betrayal of Judas. He refused to be a victim. He loved even Judas. Even in the face of the betrayal of His life, He never allowed a victim sentiment to cloud His love.

Each kept promise demonstrates His love for us—as the promises we keep demonstrate our love for others. Every other indication of love is subjectively received and is therefore equivocal. Without promise, we never really *know* that we are loved. We are little better off than the young man plucking the petals of a flower, alternating between "She loves me" and "She loves me not."

If love is no more than a feeling—if it is just subjective—what good is it? The old saw: "Love is as love does" contains a tremendous truth. True love makes itself known in action through the making and keeping of promises to others. As we shall see later in this chapter, promise is the only God-ordained bond between individuals, because promise is love in action.

Contrary to the popular mythology touted in movies and on television, our subjective feelings, even our feelings of love, never bridge the gap between us and another person *by themselves*. No one else can "feel" my feelings. No matter how strongly we feel, until that feeling compels an observable action, we cannot reach another. Feeling must be wedded to action; passion is a strong emotion *that compels action*. It is in the realm of action that we are able to reach another person and communicate our feelings. Making and keeping a promise is the prerequisite for having our feelings actually and unequivocally received by another.

In a similar way, it is only by kept promises that we know what little we can of God's vast and unsearchable character and His heart of love toward us. Promise plays an essential role in our knowledge of God. Without promise, we have only our passing, subjective feelings to indicate whether or not there is a God who loves each of us. Like the broken clock whose hands accurately tell the time twice a day, sometimes our feelings accurately reveal the love others (including God!) have for us. But often our feelings mistake love for something else—anger, indifference, harshness, and so on. Only through promise do we have a sure, *objective* basis for knowing without a doubt that God loves us.

Promise is a prominent feature of the Old Testament landscape. In Hebrew, the word we translate as "promise" means simply "word." Whenever the "word of the Lord" came to someone, it was in essence a promise. Even today we still equate making a promise with "giving our word."

In fact, "giving your word" is close to the meaning of the Latin word *promittere* from which our word "promise" evolved. *Promittere* means "to send forth." When we make a promise, we send forth our word in the fullest sense. Based on Jesus' example of the Word made flesh, our word contains our whole being. Just as Jesus is the exact reflection of the Father who sent Him, so our word incorporates all that we are for others. A promise calls out our whole being for another—everything that we have and all that we are.

We never know what a promise will require of us when we first make it. Think of the promises a husband and a wife make in marriage. Neither recognizes the totally consuming demand these promises will make on them! Even the smallest of promises sends forth our whole being. In promise, we participate in God's call to love Him with all our heart, soul, mind, and strength and our neighbor as ourselves. Martin Buber poetically described this call and Jesus' response:

> Here the *Thou* [i.e., God] appeared to the man out of deeper mystery, addressed him even out of the darkness, and he responded with his life.[13]

Both in sending forth His word to the disciples and in responding to the promises of who the Messiah was to be for God's chosen people, Jesus sent forth His whole being, entering the darkness where only God sustained Him.

In this book we are using the broadest definition of promise, much broader than the one most people are accustomed to using. We will be using promise both as a

---

[13]Martin Buber, *I and Thou*, 42.

principle and as a specific act. Behind every specific act of promising is the principle of sending forth our whole being. The principle of promise leads to specific acts of promising. When we wed the act of promising with the principle of sending forth our whole being to another, we discover a powerful dynamic of the kingdom of God; a dynamic that is nothing less than the Living God's one chosen avenue for relating to humanity. Promise is the foundation of every act God has taken toward man throughout creation.

He began by sending forth His Word to create order from the formless void. Later He sent forth Jesus, the Word made flesh. In the future He will send Him forth again as promised in Jesus' final statement in Revelation: "Yes, I am coming quickly." Promise is God's chosen method for relating with mankind from the beginning to the end of time. By adopting promise as our means of relating with others, as God does, we begin to kill the old sin nature, which relates to everyone and everything as a victim. In this and the next chapter, we will examine the nature of this ignored and forgotten principle.

In our exploration of promise, we will consider twelve propositions. Each of these describes an aspect of promise that is essential to killing the victim within. In this chapter, we will cover the first six:

1. Promise makes the invisible visible and the subjective objective.
2. Promise reveals breakdowns.
3. Promise brings order to chaos.
4. Promise generates the space for intimacy.
5. Promise connects us together in community.
6. Promise calls forth responsibility in both the one making and the one receiving the promise.

In the next chapter, we will examine an additional six propositions about promise:

7. Promise is an implicit act of faith.
8. Promise is turned into reality by the commitment behind it.
9. Promise enables us to govern ourselves in the liberty we have in Christ.
10. Promise is the key to forgiveness and repentance.
11. Promise opens up a progression of bigger possibilities.
12. Promise is the heart of reconciliation, prayer, and worship.

Promise Makes the Invisible Visible and the Subjective Objective

We use promise in the *Momentus* training as the primary tool to reveal the subjectivity of our society. During the introductory dialog with the participants, we ask them "How do you know the God of the Bible loves you." Or, "How do you know the God of Abraham, Isaac, and Jacob is the One True God?" The answers are revealing. We hear answers such as, "I just know." "The Bible says He is." "He answers my prayers." And "Through faith." Sometimes these questions just draw a blank stare. Yet we can know objectively that the God of the Bible loves us. We know He is the One True God, because He not only declared it through specific written promises, but He set about keeping them. This distinguishes Him from all other gods. Indeed, this is what it means to be True.

Promises make the invisible visible and the subjective objective. Take the word that came to Abram in a vision:

After these things the word of the LORD came to Abram in a vision, saying, "Do not fear, Abram, I am a shield to you; your reward shall be very great." And Abram said, "O Lord GOD, what wilt Thou give me, since I am childless, and the heir of my house is Eliezer of Damascus?" And Abram said, "Since Thou hast given no offspring to me, one born in my house is my heir." Then behold, the word of the LORD came to him, saying, "This man will not be your heir; but one who shall come forth from your own body, he shall be your heir." And He took him outside and said, "Now look toward the heavens, and count the stars, if you are able to count them." And He said to him, "So shall your descendants be" (Genesis 15:1-6).

Each statement God made to Abram in this passage is a promise: "your reward shall be very great," "one who shall come forth from your own body, he shall be your heir," and "so shall your descendants be [i.e., as the stars in the sky]." God's whole conversation with Abram consisted of a series of promises. Also, the promises from the Lord showed Abram God's intentions and His relationship toward him. Genesis 15:1-6 was Abram's second conversation with the Lord. The first is recorded earlier in Genesis:

Now the LORD said to Abram, "Go forth from your country, and from your relatives and from your father's house, to the land which I will show you; And *I will make you a great nation*, and *I will bless you, and make your name great; and so you shall be a blessing*; And *I will bless those who bless you, and the one who curses you I will curse. And in you all the families of the earth shall be blessed*." (Genesis 12:1-3, italics added)

This first conversation is filled with promises, too. Before the promises came, God was invisible and unseen to Abram; thus Abram's knowledge of Him could only be subjective. The promises God gave him made their relationship objective: Abram had physical criteria that allowed him to know unequivocally when the promises were fulfilled; criteria such as the birth of an heir and the proliferation of his descendants.

Just as God's promises to Abram revealed His internal, subjective feelings, our promises to others reveal our hearts. I (Dan) came face-to-face with the power of promise to reveal the invisible condition of my heart when I was about 9 years old. I had a yo-yo. It was my favorite; it was honey-colored, and smooth with shiny flecks of gold. It was perfectly balanced and fit my hand like nothing else; with it I performed many tricks. I also had a friend, a boy named Kevin, whom I loved very much. One day, in order to show him just how much I cared about him, I gave him my favorite yo-yo. He was moved by my generosity. His face lit up as he fondled the smooth, honey-colored orb. It fit his hand perfectly as well. He immediately got it to "walk the dog," go "round the world," and "rock the baby." I beamed with love for him. His joy at my gift was even more rewarding to me than owning the yo-yo had been.

Inevitably, Kevin and I got into a fight as children often do. I was livid and seized upon the yo-yo. I demanded that he return it. My fierce love had turned into even fiercer hatred. He refused. I threatened to beat him up. I was bigger and used my size to bully him. He started crying, but managed to throw the yo-yo at me before running home to mama.

The next day Kevin's mother called my father. My father sat me down on the porch of our house to hear my side of the story. Filled with my own self-righteous indignation, I proceeded to lay much of the blame for the incident squarely upon Kevin's shoulders. When I finished, he asked me to imagine what it was like for Kevin. I couldn't believe it! He had barely acknowledged my side of the story. I felt enraged by my father's request. "I don't care what it was like for Kevin," I yelled as hot tears filled my eyes, "because he doesn't care about me."

My father was unmoved by my outburst. He said, "Danny, you are being no different than Kevin. The way you are treating him is exactly the reason you are angry with him. Taking back that yo-yo is stealing. I'm going to sit here until you tell me what it was like for Kevin."

I just sat there. I felt like the world was pitted against me. Minutes passed; I said nothing and neither did my dad. My certainty that I had been wronged slowly began to crumble. When my father did not budge off the porch, I knew he meant business.

When I finally retold the story from Kevin's perspective, I began to cry about what I had done and for the black-heartedness I saw revealed in me. I wanted desperately to go to Kevin and give the yo-yo back and ask him to forgive me. I wanted to right the wrong I had done him. I never wanted anybody to treat me the way I treated Kevin. I was deeply ashamed about what had been exposed about my own heart.

Breaking my promise of friendship to Kevin symbolized by the gift of the yo-yo showed me the condition of my heart. My father was able to address my selfishness toward Kevin on the evidence of my broken promise. When I repented and returned the yo-yo, my actions once more showed Kevin the subjective shift in my heart toward him.

Promise is God's tool of revelation. Through promise He reveals Himself to us. My wife, Julie, and I (Larry) have been trying to get pregnant since we married three years ago. We had not yet resorted to medical interventions, but had all but given up hope of a normal conception—Julie had been unable to conceive for ten years.

Several months ago, we received a prophetic word—a promise—while we were visiting a church. The prophecy indicated that it was in God's plan for us to have children and that a mighty manifestation of God's power and grace would be shown to us in the next three months and we would know that the hand of God had been upon us. When we heard this prophecy, immediately we felt a subjective assurance that it was from God; plus the woman who gave us this word did not know us at all and therefore had no knowledge of our struggles and longing to have a baby. Her lack of direct knowledge of us further confirmed the word's supernatural source. We waited fully persuaded that the word was true.

Less than a month later, we traveled to Kansas City for a *Momentus* training. When we arrived, Julie went straight to bed because she was feeling tired and nauseated. The day we left for Kansas, Julie had gone to her doctor suspecting that she was pregnant. The next morning, she called home to get the results of the blood test taken the day before. Our hopes had been confirmed—her queasiness was indeed pregnancy-induced! We were elated and could barely contain our excitement; we played the tape of the prophesy for friends over and over on the phone so that they could share our joy.

Once we confirmed she was pregnant, we knew that the word we received had indeed been from the Lord. The subjective assurance became objective—what was foretold actually occurred. Whenever a promised event occurs, we have an assurance that the word was truly from God ("the word was confirmed with signs following" as Mark 16:20 says). If the promise had not come true, we would have known that it wasn't from God.

Think of Mary and the annunciation of Jesus' birth. The angel made specific promises to her:

And behold, you will conceive in your womb, and bear a son, and you shall name Him Jesus. He will be great, and will be called the Son of the Most High; and the Lord God will give Him the throne of His father David; and He will reign over the house of Jacob forever; and His kingdom will have no end (Luke 1:31-33).

Mary answered, "be it done to me according to your *word*" (Luke 1:38, emphasis added). Mary recognized the promise. In her response, Mary declared her own promise back to the angel and God. She might have said, "I am not worthy, find someone else." Instead, she chose a responsible course—she promised back that she would accept the honor God had bestowed on her. She accepted all of the consequences: telling Joseph and facing the shame of being pregnant out of wedlock, the possibility of stoning, the disapproval of friends, the knowing stares when she gave birth sooner than she should have. Mary's promise back to God to bear Jesus and everything that His birth entailed opened up the possibility for the Messiah to come to earth. Without her, or someone else like her, Jesus' birth, and therefore the perfect reflection of God to the world, would not have been possible.

The ultimate revelation of the invisible God was Jesus Himself. He said, "He who has seen Me has seen the Father," (John 14:9) and, "I and the Father are one" (John 10:30). Even more impressive than Jesus' own declarations, are the Messianic prophecies that Jesus fulfilled, many of which (such as the place of His birth, His lineage from the root of Jesse, the fact He was a Nazarene, that He was worshiped by the Magi, called out of Egypt, a man of sorrows, and many more) were outside His control and influence. A study done by professors at MIT calculated that the odds of fulfilling even six of the promises that Jesus did would be less than one in three million. Jesus fulfilled over 300 distinct prophesies about the Messiah. The possibility that these words were fulfilled by accident are beyond infinitesimal. The fulfilled promises objectively reveal Jesus as the fore-told Messiah.

Making and fulfilling promises makes the invisible God visible to us. Promise works the same for us. They make our invisible feelings and intentions visible. Until we make and keep a promise, our intentions and feelings are mysterious to others and are therefore useless. A promise made and kept demonstrates visibly in action the subjective feelings inside and the attitude of heart from which the emotions spring.

In our day, to say that feelings are useless unless a promise is made and kept seems harsh. We objectify feelings and treat them as if they have an independent existence. We treat emotions as if they were objects that we find lying around inside us. We are concerned when others ignore or hurt our feelings. Our feelings are irrelevant to others unless the feelings provoke us to action. A workaholic father may have strong emotions, he may even claim to love his sons but since he never spends time with them, he fails to make a positive difference in their lives. He has broken the inherent promises of fatherhood.

Promise makes plain the source of our emotions—whether it be self- or other-centered. Emotions can be motivated by one of two things: I can love someone because of how they make me feel or I can love them for themselves. The first springs from self-centered concerns, the second is other-centered. Promises, when fulfilled, intrude on our self-centered desires.

This power of promise to interrupt our egocentric concentration is profound, but even children readily understand it. When my (Dan's) daughter, Elizabeth, was seven, she came to me while we were picking flowers in a field behind our house and said out of nowhere, "Daddy, you love me!"

"Of course I love you, sweetheart," I said, "but why did you say that?"

She responded, "because you told me we would pick flowers and now we are—and I didn't have to remind you." I asked her what it would have meant to her if she had to remind me. "Then I would have known you were thinking of something else. I would have known that whatever you were thinking about was more important than me. You make me feel important Daddy!"

Her words knocked the wind out of me. Had I not been teaching about the power of promise just the day before? That even the smallest promises reveal the attitude of our heart toward others? Then my seven-year-old casually mentioned the truth I had struggled to communicate!

Elizabeth taught me that we reveal what really matters to us by the promises we keep—not just the promises we make. Even God demonstrates His love for us by keeping his promises and calling us to love one another. Not only is the direction of our love—toward ourselves or others—displayed in our kept promises, but we reveal our beliefs about the future whenever we make a promise.

Promise Reveals Breakdowns

Facing the future, there are only two possible relationships to take. Either we stand facing the future with faith in God's provision, or we fall into fear that God will not provide. In this fear, instead of moving forward in faith, we stop and find a way to take care of ourselves in numerous ways—perhaps by finding someone to take care of us, by exerting tyranny over ourselves and others, or by escaping through passivity, rationalizations, excuses, blame shifting, bearing judgments, or addiction. Each of these strategies is an attempt to control what is inherently uncontrollable—circumstances, other people, even God. These strategies presuppose that God will not provide; and since He will not, that we must fend for ourselves. This attitude of unbelief is the root of all sin.

In moving our focus from others to ourselves, we inevitably begin to break more and more promises. These broken promises are a type of "breakdown." In the midst of a breakdown ("breakdown" is the term we give to a broken promise or circumstances that threaten the keeping of a promise), what is missing becomes more obvious.

There are a couple of ways to hear the question, "What is missing?" A victim takes the inquiry to mean: "something is missing in me; *I* am inadequate; *I* am a failure; *I* am powerless to change the situation." The victor on the other hand sees what is missing as something she is called to provide—something missing in how she is giving herself to the others involved.

For the victor, each breakdown reveals the next step toward keeping her promise. The victim's view of the breakdown as an inadequacy within closes down the possibility for resolving it. The breakdown therefore worsens, revealing even more of the heart.

Rather than struggling to provide what is missing, we may choose to live in a fantasy, pretending that we are on our way toward fulfilling our promise. We choose to live in denial, defense, excuse, rationalization, minimization, and so on—whatever it takes to relieve the overwhelming sense of inadequacy produced from hearing "what is missing?" as if it were missing in us. This way of relating to what's missing is a breakdown because it threatens our identity. We will tend to avoid facing and admitting to breakdowns whenever our identity is at risk.

By attempting to control what is uncontrollable, we perpetuate the popular illusion that somehow life *ought* to be controllable. In the move to control beyond our power and jurisdiction, we become victims and set up an idol in the place of God. Whatever we look to for protection, whatever we find to alleviate the feeling of insecurity, becomes the idol that we worship. And then when our idols fail us, as indeed they must, we can even be a victim to our idols!

The victor on the other hand, covers himself with the shield of faith, and through being fully persuaded that all things will turn out for the good for those that love God and are called according to His purposes (Romans 8:28), stands firm on God's promises and his own promises, regardless of the circumstances.

I (Derek) was driving with Laurie and the kids in an unfamiliar town several years ago. We were heading to a popular restaurant, but had only the vaguest of directions. I was relying on my inbred compass and the feeling of being close to the goal—two directional tools with which males seem amply endowed. We were on vacation and after a busy day of sightseeing, all of us were ready to eat.

As we were driving, my feelings began to send off warnings that we were not on the right track. However, I was not about to tell Laurie. I continued to pretend that I knew where we were and where we were going.

But Laurie didn't buy it. As the minutes passed and we became more and more lost, Laurie finally asked me, "Do you know where the restaurant is?"

I answered with a noncommittal, "I think it is a few miles further on." Meanwhile the volume of whining from the back seat began to escalate.

Then came the fatal suggestion: "Let's stop and ask, just to make sure."

I ignored her, preferring to live in fantasy than admit my error by stopping to ask someone. My commitment—getting to dinner in time for our reservation—came second to looking good by *not* stopping to ask for directions. We passed four or five gas stations, probably 50 pedestrians, countless bars and pubs, convenience stores, even several police cars at fast food restaurants. Laurie finally gave up pointing out the possible ways to get directions, because I was taking each suggestion as an affront to my integrity and to real men everywhere. We ended up missing our reservation and had to wait an hour to get a table when we finally arrived, more by accident than anything else.

At the restaurant, the tension between Laurie and me increased. My sons were half-crazed with hunger. We scavenged half a dozen packages of crackers while we waited. We ordered dinner and made polite conversation about the places we had visited during the day and talked to the children. Finally the underlying tension erupted; Laurie told me how my unwillingness to stop for directions led her to feel discounted. I saw how my fear of looking bad drove Laurie away from me. By accounting for not only the specific broken promise, but also the underlying reasons that generated it, I saw the prices I paid in distance from Laurie. Men, take it from me, stopping for directions is always worth it!

Promise Brings Order to Chaos

The second law of thermodynamics, also called the law of entropy, asserts that any system's natural state—the state to which it will move—is the state with the highest degree of chaos. In the natural world, this is plainly evident: fences fall down, iron rusts, puzzle pieces get lost. Even in relationships this is easily grasped: relationships wither through lack of attention, misunderstandings escalate if unchecked, wars break out much more frequently than peace. Against this strong pull toward chaos, promise battles to establish order.

God calls us to bring order to chaos just as He did. God's first declaration in Scripture, "Let there be light," began to order creation according to the mysterious vision that He had conceived. Through His Word, the world moved from chaos to an order that conformed to His vision.

We enter a similar process whenever we make a promise. Promise begins as a vision of a future worth having with others. Then we declare the reality of what we are committed to establish. Finally, our commitment to our promise drives us to overcome every obstacle and circumstance to see the fulfillment of our vision. For Jesus, the fulfillment of his vision was joyous enough to enable Him to endure the cross.

Promise is the down payment for a future worth having; a future that is ordered based on our internal vision of it. Without promises to draw us out to one another and for others, our vision is useless. A vision must be articulated into a set of promises or it will never become reality. Nikola Tesla was an inventor who lived from 1856 to 1943. He was perhaps the most brilliant inventor of all time, far surpassing even Thomas Edison in his insight into the fundamental theories underlying his inventions. He is best known for inventing alternating current (AC), the generation and transmission of electricity with alternating current, and the AC electrical motor. Unfortunately, in addition to his inventiveness, he was a compulsive paranoid. As a result of his paranoia, he worked alone and rarely kept notes. A contemporary writer who was Tesla's friend wrote the following about an evening spent with Mark Twain and Jeffrey Johnson in Tesla's laboratory:

. . . by merely snapping his fingers [Tesla] creates instantaneously a ball of leaping red flame, and holds it calmly in his hands. As you gaze you are surprised to see it does not burn his fingers. He lets it fall upon his clothing, on his hair, into your lap, and, finally, puts the ball of flame into a wooden box. . . . Suddenly the whole laboratory was flooded with strange beautiful light . . . [Twain and Johnson] cast their eyes around the room, but found no trace of the source of the illumination.[14]

To this day, these scientific feats have never been repeated.

One of Tesla's more intriguing ideas was a plan to conduct electricity without wires using the earth as a conductor. With this system, one would stick a pole in the ground and have electrical power. Unfortunately, Tesla's vision for this system died with him, because he never wrote it down; Tesla, in spite of all the gifts he invented for mankind, was ultimately revealed as supremely selfish.

Tesla may have been a man of vision, but his vision lacked the promise to benefit mankind, thus his vision never came into actuality. Søren Kierkegaard identified living in this way as living in the despair of possibility. In this form of despair, vision exists as a possibility, but it never is united with the necessity of accomplishment. No promises are made to bring the vision into a reality. When possibility and necessity are joined, when vision and promise come together, things happen. If Tesla's idea for conducting electricity did indeed work, we will never know it, because it never was expressed as a promise—Tesla never sent himself forth to others by committing his idea to paper. Therefore, he never brought order to the chaos around him. He was duped by the thought that the internal order he generated was good enough for others, too.

---

[14]Margaret Cheney, *Tesla: Man Out of Time*, 3-4.

The existentialism of our age tells us that what matters is the intention, the idea or thought, not the actuality. But even the best idea has no value unless it becomes a reality in the physical universe. How many good ideas do each of us have in a week or a month? How many of these good ideas ever become a reality? The difference between good ideas and their realization is in the declaring of promises.

Unfortunately, once we make a promise, circumstances immediately arise which threaten to confound us. To endure the chaos as circumstances shift we must cling to the relationship we are committed to having with God and others. While writing this book, my (Derek's) third son, Tristan, was born. As any parent knows, infants present new circumstances to challenge the vision of the relationship you would have with them. Tristan is no exception. Just as I climb into bed, Tristan wakes up—no matter what the hour. Decision time—do I act from frustration or do I act from my vision of loving my son and building a lifelong relationship worth having? The intrusion of circumstance threatens every vision, attempting to reassert the dominance of chaos.

Promise Generates the Space for Intimacy

In addition to ordering chaos according to one's inner vision, promise creates an environment of intimacy. Intimacy is built not only through the process of making and keeping promises, but also in accounting for broken promises. If we account honestly for our failure in keeping promises, we reveal the inner workings of our souls to the ones to whom we sent ourselves, but did not reach. This generates a deep intimacy.

Often our accounting for broken promises provokes the ones with whom we are accounting to consider the attitude of their own hearts that may have hindered us from fulfilling our promise.

During a *Momentus* training, I (Derek) had several heated exchanges with a participant. I was committed that this woman would receive the love that I had for her. I was committed to reach her with my love, but no matter what I did, my love didn't get through. I ranted and raved; was quiet and calm; I kidded with her. Nothing seemed to work. I found myself confused and frustrated. I expected her to receive my love; at times I was even tempted to blame her—it was her problem in receiving love, not mine in sending it. Confusion and frustration often result when circumstances do not match my expectations of how God or others should respond to me.

It soon became clear to me that I reminded this woman of someone in her life with whom she was bitter. My frustration built to the point that I wanted to give up. Verging on despair, I accounted for all that was separating me from her: my frustration, anger, arrogance, and harshness. I then asked forgiveness for not communicating my love effectively. My willingness to account in this way created the intimacy that nothing else had.

In the midst of confusion, promise provides the compass for directing us through seemingly overwhelming circumstances. The question: "Did my promise come to pass?" provides direction in which to take action. Whatever action we take next may not be our last to fulfill our promise. But over and over again, our promise draws us to take action until our promise is a reality. We can overcome any circumstance or any challenge with repeated committed action.

Saul of Tarsus was a Pharisee in Israel during and after Jesus' ministry. As a strict Pharisee, his promise was to obey the law, thinking that therein he would give glory of God. He regarded the upstart Christian sect as a threat to Judaism and determined to work to eradicate the Christians. Furthermore, he received the authority from the high priest to capture and imprison Christians and was actively living his commitment to God. It was in fact as he was pursuing his vision that the risen Christ apprehended him on the road to Damascus. His conversion and subsequent ministry as Paul the Apostle bore tremendous fruit.

Another great example is the four leprous men during the siege of Samaria by the Arameans. The siege had led to a famine. The four lepers decided that one way or another they would die, so they might as well take their chances with the enemy, who at least had food. When they got up and took action, they found that the Arameans had fled in fear from the imagined sound of an army. We see a great lesson in these accounts.

Only as we travel the road toward our vision can God redirect us. Had Saul stayed in the strict confines of the Pharisee's life in Jerusalem, he would not have encountered Jesus on the road. If the lepers had remained to die by the gate, no one would have found out about the empty Aramean camp (II Kings 7:5). We must trust that God will direct our steps as we whole-heartedly pursue the work to which we believe we are called. The man sitting at home every night in front of the TV waiting for something to happen is probably not the man getting visions of the Lord Jesus!

Promise Connects Us Together in Community

In every role in our lives, the explicit and implicit promises we make define who we are for others. Likewise, the promises that others make define who they are for us. The explicit and implicit promises of marriage define the roles of husband or wife and distinguish the marriage relationship from all other types of relationships. A fireman is distinct from a policeman based on his promises—a fireman promises to put out fires and a policeman promises to catch criminals.

The implicit promises define the roles in which we live. By virtue of being a husband and father, a man bears a set of implicit promises to his wife and children. These implicit promises bind him to his family. The explicit promises that a man makes to his family, however small, are added to the implicit promises. Taken together, all of our promises make us unique. For others, the legacy we leave them is the totality of the promises we have made and kept. Promises make us distinct *from* others; they also bind us *to* others.

The way promise binds is evident in the definition found in *Webster's Dictionary of the American Language*:

> A declaration, written or verbal, made by one person to another, that binds the person who makes it either in honor, conscience, or law to do or forebear a certain act. It gives the one to whom it is made the right to expect or claim the performance or forbearance of the act specified.

According to Webster, promises bind us in either honor, conscience, or law. Honor refers to the social realm—the realm of our reputation and our good name. We are bound to perform or forbear the promised act in order to maintain and enhance our reputation. Because we value our reputation, we act consistently with that reputation. Honor is the ledger that continually measures our reputation with people—when we keep or break our word, we either add or subtract from the ledger.

Honor is also the realm in which we publicly glorify God. As a Christian, our public persona is to be a reflection of Jesus to the world. Our honor therefore honors God. As Christians, how we keep promises reflects God's love for the world.

The ancient Hebrew language did not recognize the Greek and Roman delineation of spirit, soul, and body. Rather, they divided the self into the inner and outer. The Hebrews used two words which are both translated as 'soul' in English: *shem*, used to designate the public self, and *nephesh*, which designates the inner self. Webster's definition of promise uses these similar categories of inner and outer self. Honor is the realm of the *shem*: who we are for others and the expectation placed on us based on our position, roles, and duties.

The *nephesh* is our inner sense of identity—who we are to ourselves as compared to who we are for others. This is the realm of the conscience—our internal sense of right and wrong, of what is appropriate and inappropriate. Our conscience is the God-given faculty for discerning right and wrong in our own actions. When no one is around, our *honor* is not at stake, but our conscience still binds us to our promise. Our conscience is not an absolute measure however. It can be seared to the point of numbness on the one hand, or educated and made more sensitive. Conscience is the last line of defense when we are alone; only our conscience restrains us when honor and our public reputation (or a law enforcement officer) do not. It is our conscience that holds us back from hopping a fence into an orchard and plucking apples without the owner's permission.

The third realm of promise is the civil realm, the realm in which civil laws are passed to maintain liberty for the populace. Here we are bound to others because of an explicit set of promises regarding conduct that are formalized into laws.

The idea that promise binds us to others runs contrary to our cultural thinking. Most of us believe emotions are the ties that bind. Our emotions, by definition, are fluid—their intensity waxes and wanes. They flood over and through each other like waves on the sea. When we take our emotions as our bond to others, we place ourselves in a precarious position:

at any moment we can be toppled over by the next emotional wave. As children mature, they must face this insecurity. I (Derek) remember when my son began realizing that my occasional frustration and anger at his actions did not change how we were bound to each other. He was three and a half years old and loved to push the button on our garage door opener. One day, as he and I were leaving to run some errands, he pressed the button to close the garage door when the car was only half way out. The garage door came down on the car and dented and scratched the hood of the car. I was furious! I stopped the car, grabbed the opener from his hands, and stormed out of the car. After a few minutes, I came back in. Reed was crying. I realized he had not intended to damage the car, he was just excited by the power of opening and shutting the big garage door. I asked him to forgive me and told him what I was feeling—that I was angry that the car was dented, but that the anger was at myself for not seeing that he might hit the button early. As we were talking, he began to relax; he realized that my connection to him—I doubt he thought of it in terms of implicit promises—was bigger than my emotions, both of love and of anger. After that incident, he began to express more freely his upset, hurt, and angry emotions to me as well.

Emotions are the *result* of how we relate to God and others. Promise, on the other hand, is our declaration of *how* we are committed to relating to God and others. As we live our promises, our emotional life tells us a great deal about our relationship to God and others. Emotions are the result of our beliefs colliding or coinciding with reality—with events outside of ourselves. They arise from how our beliefs, expectations and hopes line up with the actualities of the physical world. Promise pierces through our behavior and through our emotions to reveal the beliefs that are at the core of our souls.

Just as promise binds us to another through a claim on our actions, unforgiveness binds us as well, but in a different way. By harboring unforgiveness against someone, we bind ourselves tightly to them and the unforgiveness soon turns into bitterness, which extinguishes love. C. S. Lewis wrote about this transformation of heart:

> Love anything, and your heart will certainly be wrung and possibly be broken. If you want to make sure of keeping it intact, you must give your heart to no one, not even to an animal. Wrap it carefully round with hobbies and little luxuries; avoid all entanglements; lock it up safe in the casket or coffin of your selfishness. But in that casket—safe, dark, motionless, airless—it will change. It will not be broken; it will become unbreakable, impenetrable, irredeemable. The alternative to tragedy, or at least to the risk of tragedy, is damnation. The only place outside of Heaven where you can be perfectly safe from all the dangers and perturbations of love is Hell.
>
> I believe that the most lawless and inordinate loves are less contrary to God's will than a self-invited and self-protective lovelessness.[15]

As we shall see in the next chapter, forgiveness allows us to set the other person free from the bonds of bitterness which result from broken promises.

---

[15]C. S. Lewis, *The Four Loves*, 169-170.

Promise Calls Forth Responsibility in Both the One Making and the One Receiving the Promise

In our culture, we have leveled the meaning of responsibility to such an extent that responsibility is indistinguishable from guilt and fault. When we ask, "Who's responsible?" we usually mean "Who's at fault?" But fault has nothing to do with responsibility; it is responsibility's antithesis.

Fault is concerned with justifying what was not done and how I was right or wrong for what I did or didn't do. Admitting fault is often just an admission of guilt which inevitably leads to justification, self-preservation, and idolatry.

Fault belongs to a paradigm including blame, shame, and credit. In this paradigm, the focus is on what a person can get from a situation. If the outcome turns out well, we take credit. If the results are poor, we level blame at others or shame at ourselves. Blame, shame, and credit comprise the paradigm of idolatry and the attitude of heart of a master, not a servant.

Responsibility, on the other hand, belongs to the paradigm of promise. Rather than being concerned with what we can get from a person or a situation, responsibility directs us toward what we can give, how we can send ourselves forth to others to see that their promise is *realized*. Responsibility drives us to account for results as they happen—not for the purpose of assigning blame or taking credit, but to make adjustments so that we accomplish our commitment or goal. Responsibility means accounting for the relationship we take to our actions; that is, to notice when we are relating as a victim and indulging in circumstance-driven rationalizations for our lack of results.

A scripture that exemplifies the essence of responsibility is found in the Sermon on the Mount:

Again, you have heard that the ancients were told, 'You shall not make false vows [i.e., promises], but shall fulfill your vows to the Lord.' But I say to you, make no oath at all, either by heaven, for it is the throne of God, or by the earth, for it is the footstool of His feet, or by Jerusalem, for it is THE CITY OF THE GREAT KING. Nor shall you make an oath by your head, for you cannot make one hair white or black. But let your statement be, 'Yes, Yes' or 'No, No'; and anything beyond these is of [the evil one]. (Matthew 5:33-37)

In modern society, we rarely talk about making oaths, which you might think is a good thing according to this scripture. However, whenever we are operating from the victim's paradigm of blame, shame, and credit, we are engaged in the same thing as making oaths, even if we don't call it that.

The definition of oath from Webster's Collegiate Dictionary reads:

A solemn usually formal calling upon God or a god to witness to the truth of what one says or to witness that one sincerely intends to do what one says; a solemn attestation of the truth or inviolability of one's words; something (as a promise) corroborated by an oath; a form of expression used in taking an oath.

We run into oaths most frequently at the installation ceremonies of public officials. I have no qualms about the civil use of oaths; my concern is the attitude of the heart, which would strengthen a promise with an oath. Adding an oath to a promise is sowing tares directly in with the wheat!

An oath is distinct from a promise; indeed an oath is a way for a person to bolster the strength of a promise by calling on someone or something else to witness or insure that the promise will be kept. The oaths of office taken by public officials include calling on God to empower the officeholder to uphold his duties.

An oath is an admission that our word and promise are not sufficient—we must appeal to more than the promise itself for it to be believed or to be fulfilled. An oath impugns the word of the one making it. Why swear by our head, when we cannot change even the color of one hair? Why indeed, when we *do* have the power to accomplish our promise. Oaths set up a huge excuse: a backdoor to justification. Think of the traditional oath in court: "I solemnly swear to tell the truth, the whole truth, and nothing but the truth so help me God." The oath, "so help me God," gives me a ready excuse for not telling the truth—God did not give me sufficient help. It's His fault!

The person who resorts to oaths is like Chanticleer the rooster who thought he caused the sun to rise with his crowing. How surprised he was when the sun came up one morning when he forgot to crow! Swearing by something or someone to strengthen a promise is similar—the oath, like the rooster, has nothing to do with the promise being accomplished.

Oaths are unnecessary and foster an unwarranted sense of security, which comes from surrendering responsibility to other people and things. Oaths create a victim mentality by presupposing that our word and promise are insufficient in themselves, that they need a shot in the arm to be effective. Oaths become a crutch.

Matthew quotes Jesus as saying, "But let your statement be, 'Yes, Yes' or 'No, No'; anything beyond these is of [the evil one.]" He is saying that our word and promise stand alone; they need no assistance. Then Jesus adds the remarkable phrase that "anything else is of the evil one." Anything else is like Satan.

Now this sounds extreme—does Jesus really mean that using an oath is like Satan? The oath, "So help me God" sounds like appeal to His provision.

Adding an oath to your promise represents the pattern of all temptation and the entry point for sin and evil. Not only is the oath, "so help me God," not a request for divine assistance, it implies the opposite—it implies, as all oaths do, that God has not provided, that we need something from the outside to make us complete and must go out and get it. When we lean on our own strength, we determine the state of our internal being, our *nephesh,* on the external appearance of things.

This is the pattern of the original sin in the Garden of Eden, as recorded in Genesis:

> And the Lord God commanded the man, saying, "From any tree of the garden you may eat freely; but from the tree of the knowledge of good and evil you shall not eat, for in the day that you eat from it you shall surely die". . . . Now the serpent was more crafty than any beast of the field which the Lord God had made. And he said to the woman, "Indeed, has God said, 'You shall not eat from any tree of the garden'?" And the woman said to the serpent, "from the fruit of the trees of the garden we may eat; but from the fruit of the tree which is in the middle of the garden, God has said, 'You shall not eat from it or touch it, lest you die.'" And the serpent said to the woman, "You surely shall not die! For God knows that in the day you eat from it your eyes will be opened, and you will be like God, knowing good and evil." (Genesis 2:16-1, 3:1-5)

The underlying presumption was that God was withholding something from Adam and Eve, that they needed the fruit of the tree of the knowledge of good and evil to be complete. Adam and Eve knew that they had been made in the image of

God; that was no secret to them. But consider the thinking that preceded the Fall: Adam and Eve were snared by the thought that they needed something else, something beyond what God had already provided, to make up for a lack that God had created in them. They presupposed that God had set them up to fail.

The choice of right and wrong was absolutely, unequivocally clear to Adam and Eve before the Fall. The temptation of the serpent to Adam and Eve comes down to believing that God short-changed them and cheated them, and that, as a consequence, they needed something that they had to go out and get for themselves.

If Adam had been responsible, in terms of the root meaning of "promising back," he would have held to his implicit promise to Eve to fight for what was best for her. He would have clung to God's promise that he was made in God's image and had dominion over the Evil One. He would have risked losing Eve and made himself a ransom for her, rather than joining her in sin.

Adam was deceived by the lust of his own heart. Satan has no power with us except when we harbor lust in out hearts. Adam was willing to go along with Eve because he too believed that God would not provide for him.

The one receiving a promise has the responsibility to assess the commitment that is sent along with the promise. Imagine that you have asked to borrow a friend's car for the weekend. She agrees, but requests that you return the car by Sunday night so that she can go to work Monday morning. If you tell her, "Sure, no problem—I will have the car back to you Sunday night if I feel up to it," she would be crazy to expect the car to be back Sunday night. The test of responsibility is the promise that is sent back. To be responsible, your friend would have to clarify that the promise was not contingent on whether you felt like returning the car or not: "Hey, I don't care what you feel like, will you return the car Sunday night by 9 pm?"

Every promise invites the one to whom it is made to promise back—to assess the commitment that comes with the promise. A broken promise is a cry for help, rather than a reason to be offended. Whenever we are offended because someone did not keep their promise to us, it is an indication that we were not relating responsibly.

An associate of mine (Derek's) promised to have a project completed in two weeks. We agreed to check in with each other in a week. By the end of the week, neither of us had called. I noticed the broken agreement but sat back waiting for *him* to call *me*. Three days after the week ended I finally called him. He didn't return my call. Now I began to get offended, but realized that I had not been responsible. When we agreed to check in with each other, I had assumed that he would call me. I could have seen his not calling me as a signal that he needed help, but I did not because I was more concerned with justifying my own slack attitude and was frankly feeling superior for having been the only one to call.

A pastor in New Mexico became concerned when a number of his parishioners went through the *Momentus* training. He called me (Dan) to communicate these concerns. The way he triangulated me into his discussion of people in his own church immediately set off my conscience. It struck me as irresponsible that he involved me in issues that could only be resolved in conversation with the people with whom he had issues. I wondered why he was addressing me rather than his parishioners. His biggest concern was the degree of liberty that these graduates expressed. These graduates of our training had become more intimate and expressed the intimacy through hugging. Somehow the pastor thought this was something that we taught, rather than a spontaneous expression of intimacy.

As we talked, the pastor mentioned that he was concerned about the hugging from a sexual standpoint. From that point in the conversation, he spoke less about the training and more about the personal issues and struggles he was in. He admitted that he never counseled a woman alone because he feared his own lust. By the end of our conversation, I realized that rather than dealing with the root issue—his lust—he preferred to control the outward circumstances—how and when he met with women.

In fact, his whole quarrel with the graduates of *Momentus* had very little to do with them and much more to do with his own struggle with lust. He used his position to get on his soapbox. He violated his implicit promise to his parishioners to separate his own issues from theirs. His irresponsibility echos Paul's question posed in his letter to the Corinthians, "why is my freedom judged by another's conscience?" (I Corinthians 10:29).

5. Promise—Sending Your Heart To Others

Do nothing from selfishness or empty conceit, but with humility of mind let each of you regard one another as more important than himself.

Philippians 2:3

Every promise we make calls us out of ourselves. The call is not to some principle or idea; it is to reach someone else with our heart and love—to establish with another the quality of relationship that meets the deepest longings of our hearts.

As we saw in the last chapter, promise is the key to living together as a community. Promise also impacts the central issues of life: faith, responsibility, liberty, forgiveness, repentance, progressing toward a vision, reconciliation, prayer, and worship.

Promise Is an Implicit Act of Faith

Promise is not made in a vacuum but creates expectations in those to whom we make them. When I expect a promise to be fulfilled, I organize my life accordingly. Because Abram expected God to fulfill his promises, he left Ur of the Chaldeans. He left his country, his forefathers, his immediate family, and friends. Abram staked his life and the lives of those who went with him on God's promise to make his descendants a great nation.

Even simple promises give rise to expectations. When a casual friend calls you to set up a breakfast meeting, she creates an expectation in you and you begin to organize your life. You mark your calendar, set your alarm, make sure you have gas in your car; you do not promise the same time to others, because you mean to keep your word. You surmount every obstacle to your being there as agreed, and your friend does the same.

Abram's expectation was met in the provision of God's promise. He and his family not only survived, but prospered—living in the expectation of the fulfillment of God's word.

How often do we consider how many people we impact when we either break or keep a promise? How many people can prosper in the provision of our word?

I (Dan) was involved in a committee at church that fed homeless people at the local fire station. Each family on the committee promised to prepare a meal once a month. I was traveling on the East Coast when I retrieved a phone message from the man who was scheduled to feed the poor that week. His message said that his wife was pregnant and sick, so he wouldn't be able to fulfill his promise. I called him back immediately to tell him I couldn't switch with him because I was out of town. He said he didn't care, he wasn't going to fulfill his agreement. In my hotel room, I thought of the homeless people expecting a meal that day. I knew that they were depending on the provision of our word. So I got on the phone and made enough calls and requests of others until the obligation was fulfilled. The man who canceled was not considering the impact his promise made on others. He was not thinking about the people who expected the provision that his word offered. Rather he was concerned about himself and his circumstances.

Living in the expectation of someone's word calls for faith—from both the sender of the promise and the receiver. If receiving a promise is an act of faith, making a promise is one too. We have no assurance that we'll even be alive to fulfill the promises we make. Barring a fatal accident, promise still requires faith because we don't know what circumstances we must handle in order to fulfill our promises.

Faith is called out of each of us when we face the circumstances that hinder fulfilling of our promises. Faith is one facet of how we send ourselves forth in our promise. We send everything in us when we make a promise, we put ourselves at stake for our promises to be fulfilled. Being at stake in our own promises tempts us to become offended when someone breaks a promise to us. Depending on whether we see ourselves as a master or servant, a broken promise will become to us either a reason to be offended or a cry for help. If in a particular moment I am relating to those around me as a master—focused on myself and how others are treating me—I will be offended when someone breaks his promise to me. On the other hand, if I am focused on being a servant in that moment—one who loves his neighbor as himself—I will not become offended, but will be willing to consider what the other person is battling; what he is up against to prompt him to break his promise. A master treats all those around him as objects to serve his will. A servant realizes that everyone he meets is an individual to love; an individual with his own concerns, hopes, dreams, disappointments, and heartaches. Our attitude of heart—either master or servant—determines how we react to a broken promise.

I (Derek) have a friend who is habitually late for our meetings, sometimes by as much as an hour. I recently realized that I had become indifferent to her. I neither became offended at her repeated broken agreements, nor did I pursue what was going on in her life to prompt her to break her promises. In becoming indifferent to my friend, I treated her as an object. I discounted her word by modifying my expectations. I had judged her as incapable of being on time. When I finally recognized my indifference, I knew that I needed to address and reconcile our relationship. Who was she for me that I was willing to be indifferent to her? What did I need to share with her that I had withheld from her? When I sat down with her, I still had to overcome a feeling of helplessness, a feeling that no matter what I did, my friend wouldn't hear me. I confessed to my friend the indifference I harbored against her. She responded with a nod and the comment, "I have felt a distance between us . . . also an unwillingness on my part to do anything about it." She then asked me to forgive her for the times she had been late. By airing our judgments and pain, a new relationship of trust and forgiveness was established. A corollary benefit of tackling the breakdown with my friend was that I experienced a new freedom with God as well. My indifference to my friend was a reflection of my indifference to God. By shifting the attitude of my heart toward my friend, I shifted my relationship with God.

My righteousness or my "right-relatedness" with my friend was based on my willingness to trust God. My honesty risked the whole relationship—she might have become offended and never talked to me again. My trust in God was revealed by my sitting down with her to talk about my indifference. Responding to a promise requires faith; faith in turn allows for the possibility for righteousness. Abram is a great example.

The expectation of the fulfillment of God's promise that Abram would have a son was the foundation of his faith. Abram's response of faith to God's promises in Genesis 15:6 resulted in righteousness: "Then he [Abram] believed in the LORD, and He reckoned it to him as righteousness." The expectation leads to specific action. What opened up righteousness for Abram was his willingness to take action based on the expectation of God's fulfillment of His promises.

Promise is turned into reality by the commitment behind it

In an advertisement, Shearson Lehman Brothers defined commitment in this way:

> Commitment is what transforms a promise into a reality; it is the words that speak boldly of your intentions, and the actions that speak louder than words. Commitment is the stuff character is made of; the power to change the face of things. It is the daily triumph of integrity over skepticism!

The word "commitment" shares the same root word in Latin as promise; the literal translation is "to send with." Commitment is the strength of character that drives us to go the second mile, and the third, and the fourth mile if needed, in order to keep our promise.

Commitment is the determination of will that is *sent with* a promise. Determination is the singular focus on the will of God, demonstrated by Jesus in the Garden of Gethsemane as he struggled with the coming crucifixion. He wanted, if possible, to avoid it. He agonized over the thought of it—to the point that he sweated, as it were, great drops of blood (Luke 22:44). In the face of the coming agony and turmoil, His determination to follow the Father's will and not His own will carried Him through.

The prices we pay to keep the promises we make reveal the commitment motivating us. As a young man in my early twenties, I (Dan) was making lots of money owning and brokering movie theaters. My own pleasure and gratification were the focus of my life— I governed my life to satisfy myself.

As a result of my commitment to self-gratification, I developed an addiction to cocaine.

I remained addicted even after an intense conversion experience when I was 23. In fact, I managed to integrate my addiction with my Christianity by reading the Bible while I was high on cocaine. After I married my wife Aileen in 1980, I continued to use drugs. Six months later, I was in a head-on collision while driving on the highway one night. My first awareness after the crash was of being in a comfortable state, similar to being just between sleep and wakefulness. I felt Jesus stroking His fingers through my hair. He asked me, "Do you want to stay with me or go back to work? You have much work left to do." I told Him that I wanted to go back. I woke up in the car with the steering wheel in my chest and broken glass strewn everywhere. Sirens were blaring and the lights of the emergency vehicles flashed all around me.

When I reached the hospital, I was in extreme trauma. Both my lungs were collapsed; I had a crushed femur and jaw; I had sustained damage to my pancreas, spleen, and stomach. My heart stopped three times. The doctors expected me to be in the hospital two years—one in intensive care and one in recovery and rehabilitation. During exploratory surgery, the doctors removed my spleen and appendix. They decided to wait to operate on my leg and put me on morphine.

After six days, I had another vision of Jesus. He told me to stop the morphine, to get off the breather, and to start reading the Bible. My leg was operated on after 11 days rather than the doctor's original estimate of four months. I left the hospital in 18 days.

My addiction to cocaine stopped for a while after coming home from the hospital. My son was born six months later, which furthered my resolve to stay away from drugs. However, a few months later, I found myself in a full-blown addiction again. I had not yet changed from seeking self-gratification to seeking to serve others.

My *metanoia* came four months later. One rainy night I was reading the Gospel of John while snorting cocaine. I would read a few lines, then pray and meditate. As I had my eyes closed, I saw a vision of Aileen and Danny as a five-year-old, walking hand in hand away from me. Aileen turned back to me and said, "You could have been his father." Suddenly I saw a vision of Danny as a teenager, snorting coke and doing drugs. He looked wretched and despairing.

I opened my eyes and looked down at the Bible. My eyes landed on John 3:16, "For God so loved the world, that He gave his only begotten Son, that whoever would believe in Him would not perish but have eternal life." I suddenly felt a deep pain and sorrow for how much I was hurting the Father. It wasn't shame or guilt, but rather remorse for the pain I was causing Him. I stood up, walked outside, and dumped the cocaine out on the lawn in the rain.

The next morning I entered a detoxification program in Wilbur Hot Springs, California. I stopped using drugs cold turkey from that point on and entered the struggle to live responsibly. What made the difference this time was the shift in my commitment—from my own gratification to loving my heavenly Father and my family for the sake of our future together.

Addiction is a terrible and relentless enemy. I thank God that I have only lapsed once in the twelve years of my sobriety. Unfortunately that one lapse was with Carl about 18 months after I left the detox program. There was something about being with him in that same environment that made it seem natural. I willingly gave myself as a victim to the "naturalness" of the situation in order to get high. I wasn't thinking of my impact on Carl. Instead of contributing to his life, I feel like I hurried his death. "Changing the face of things" takes every emotional and physical resource and, even then, traps and pitfalls are inevitable. The test of a transformation is the dedication to keep at it over and over again.

This type of commitment drove Thomas Edison. When Edison set out to invent the light bulb, the prospect of a small electric lamp was the holy grail of electrical research. The only electric lights to date were huge arc lamps that put out hundreds of thousands of watts—suitable for the World's Fair and little else. Edison had a vision of replacing the ubiquitous gas lamps that lit houses and city streets with a similar network of electrical lights; small, portable lights that would be turned on and off with the flip of a switch. He saw his vision with such certainty that he had the *chutzpa* to announce his intentions to the press before he even began. He invited reporters to visit his laboratory and told them exactly what he was going to invent.

After the fanfare of his announcement died down, Edison began his work. He tried over 10,000 different materials without finding one that worked the way he had envisioned. In the process, Edison used whatever emotion he was experiencing to further his vision. At first, it was the thrill of the hunt. After the first several thousand experiments, the emotion switched to the desire to avoid humiliation, then to boredom and a desire to move on to other projects. He used the emotions of the moment to drive himself toward accomplishing the vision he stated in his promise. By promising the entire world he would invent the incandescent light bulb, he put himself, his reputation, and his honor at risk. His commitment carried him through years of trial and error, through disappointment, ridicule, and doubt, until he finally came up with a filament that made the light bulb work. What a difference his discipline and passion, his promise, vision, and commitment made for the world!

The restraint Edison practiced was rooted in his vision. As Proverbs says: "Where there is no vision, the people are unrestrained" (Proverbs 28:19). Vision brings constraint—a directing of the will and passions toward the envisioned outcome.

Commitment safeguards the sacred property of our name and reputation. When we place a high value on what binds us to another—our honor, our conscience, and our integrity with civil law—our reputation remains intact and we have all that we need.

On the other hand, if we falter in our commitment and we lose our honorable name and reputation, we are more abject than a penniless beggar. Commitment is the singleness of heart and mind that overcomes every obstacle to fulfill the promises we have made for our name's sake and the sake of the ones to whom our promise went forth. We glorify God's name when we keep a promise, because we take part in His express nature.

Promise Enables Us to Govern Ourselves in the Liberty We Have in Christ

As Christians, we enjoy the liberty that is promised us in the Scripture: "where the Spirit of the Lord is, there is liberty." Our liberty is absolute. As the Apostle Paul wrote, "All things are lawful, but not all things are profitable. All things are lawful, but not all things edify" (I Corinthians 10:23). We are free to do anything we want. We are free to run for President, to start a church, to panhandle on the street corner; we can even commit crimes. Nothing external restrains us. An infinite array of possibilities face each of us. The questions are, what do we do with this liberty and how do we govern ourselves in the liberty we have?

This is the focus of the question, "Who or what is in control?" Liberty implies that we have the power to choose. The way we govern ourselves can be reduced to three categories: 1) to govern ourselves by our promises, 2) to govern ourselves by arbitrary self-will, or 3) to abdicate our power to choose and let chance, circumstances, or someone else decide.

Promise, self-will, or circumstances: these summarize our choices. Promise is the way of the victor; self-will and circumstances the way of the victim.

The way of a victor turns the table on our normal tendency to judge ourselves subjectively and everyone else objectively. Rather than always giving himself leeway because of his subjective intentions, the victor governs himself by his objective promises. Making a promise declares the objective standard that we choose to apply to ourselves.

This is an essential property of promise—it is not imposed from an external source, but from our own choice. Once we make a promise, it becomes the objective standard for our behavior. Our promises also become invitations for others to contribute to our lives.

For example, I (Dan) promised a friend that I would attend a fund-raising event for her non-profit organization, but I recorded the wrong date in my calendar. She was well connected in fund-raising circles and several well-known Christian leaders would be there whom she wanted me to meet. When the day came for the fundraiser and I did not arrive, she called me to find out where I was. When I heard her voice on the phone, something clicked inside and my stomach fell to the floor—before she even said it, I knew that the fund raiser was that day, a three-hour drive away. On the phone, I had the impulse to cover my mistake with a lie: I told her that a family crisis had come up, but said I would make the awards banquet that night.

Aileen heard me lie and confronted me on it. I wanted to slant my explanation with her, too, but I paused for a moment and saw a vision of what the future would be like—covering up one lie with another—lie upon lie stretching off into the future. I even began to give a rationalization: "Aileen you don't understand . . . ." But the words dried up. As I thought about the compromise Aileen would have to make in order to cover for my lie, I began to cry. I knew I had to break the hold of this lie by confessing to my friend. I didn't want to admit my error and look bad in front of her because I believed she had the financial contacts to help my ministry grow. The lie I told proved my lack of faith in God's power to redeem me in spite of my broken promise. For three hours in the car I rehearsed ways to confess to her. When I saw her upon arriving, I grabbed her and pulled her to the side of the room. With my heart in my throat and tears in my eyes, I confessed my lie and asked her to forgive me. She smiled and said, "Okay, Dan. I do forgive you." Relief flooded through me.

Had I not made the initial promise to my friend, I would have missed the opportunity to see the lack of trust in my heart. My broken promise made the attitude of my heart visible.

A promise has the following characteristics:

1) It is a public declaration *between two or more* people. Note that promises made to oneself are not promises, they are resolutions.

2) It is time-specific and contained in time; it has a beginning, a middle, and an end.

3) It has specific, objective conditions of fulfillment.

These characteristics restrain rebellion and arbitrary self-will. Arbitrary self-will is governing your choices by the subjective desire of the moment. For example, if you agree to meet a friend for dinner at 6:00 pm Thursday and then choose to go to the movies with another friend without renegotiating the first dinner appointment, you are practicing arbitrary self-will.

Some would say that governing ourselves by promise is a prescription for anarchy. This is not true. Self-government is entirely consistent with living under the auspices of civil government. To govern ourselves does not exclude obeying the civil authorities; in fact, obeying civil government is an expression of the implicit promises each of us carries as a citizen of our homeland. Our self-government, however, does not depend on a just civil government. Even in the most oppressive civil governments, we still have complete liberty to govern ourselves. Examples abound of men and women living in freedom despite authoritarian and oppressive governments. Richard Wurmbrand in Communist Rumania and Victor Frankl in the Nazi concentration camp environment are premier examples. Both Wurmbrand and Frankl learned through their experiences that when all else is taken away, the last human freedom is the freedom to choose how to relate to circumstances. In other words, the last human freedom is the freedom to choose to be a victim or to be a victor.

Daniel, under the rule of Nebuchadnezzar, lived freely under an oppressive civil government. Daniel and his compatriots stood for their beliefs in the faith that God would deliver them, and He did. He preserved Shadrach, Meshach, and Abed-nego from the midst of the blazing furnace; and preserved Daniel from the lion's den.

Not only does our own self-government not depend on the civil government, our dependence runs the other way. The character of society's overall self-government determines the nature of the civil government. The civil government, which Abraham Lincoln called "government of the people, by the people, for the people," can have no more integrity than its constituent members. In contrast, our government views itself as existing above the people. Rather than serving the people, the common belief in the U.S. is that people are here to serve the government.

Benjamin Franklin recognized this dependence of the government on the character of the people. In a speech before the Constitutional Convention, in which he supported the Constitution even though he thought it flawed, he said,

> I think . . . there is no Form of Government but what may be a Blessing to the People if well administered; and I believe farther that this [Constitution] is likely to be well administered for a course of years, and can only end in Despotism as other Forms have done before it, when the People shall become so corrupted as to need Despotic Government, being incapable of any other.[16]

Despotism is a system of government in which the ruler has absolute power. It can only occur when the people accept the absolute, external rule; when they give up their rights and choose to be victims. Recall what Frederick Douglass wrote:

> Find out just what people will submit to and you have found the exact amount of injustice and wrong which will be imposed upon them; and these will continue until they are resisted with either words or blows, or with both. The limits of tyrants are prescribed by the endurance of those whom they oppress.[17]

---

[16]Speech before the Constitutional Convention, September 17, 1787.

[17]Letter to Gerrit Smith, March 30, 1849.

A remarkable mystery is that the way we relate to the promises we have made is a reflection of the way we relate to God. Why would this be true? Why would our relationship with God be reflected in the relationship we take to the promises we make?

The common grounding point is that both relationships call us to reveal the provision upon which we depend. One of God's names is Jehovah-Jireh or "God the Provider." *God has declared Himself to be Provider.* Our response to this declaration is either faith or disbelief. If we choose the latter and do not depend on God's provision, we depend on some other source—ourselves, other people, the government, or circumstances—to provide for us.

When we make a promise, the relationship we take to the promise reflects the relationship we are taking to God in that moment. If we are trusting in God's provision, we will believe we have the ability to fulfill our promise. If we are looking to anyone or anything else to be the provision, we will be a victim instead of a victor. When we keep our promises only because it feels good or we don't have any better options, we reveal a relationship with God that is based on convenience—His concerns are ours as long as we have no better options. If we refrain from promising for fear of not keeping a promise, we reveal our view that God is a punishing judge who will not provide for us. If we make promises and continually break them, without a thought to our reputation or conscience, we reveal the shallow depth of our relationship with the Lord. We take His name in vain, because we call ourselves Christians yet do not adopt His concerns.

How we relate to the promises we make is a clear reflection of our relationship with God. Furthermore, if the source of our provision is anyone other than God, we create an idol as the alternative source of our provision. Jesus kept every promise He implicitly and explicitly made that reveals His perfect communion and reflection of the Father. In making promises we have the opportunity to govern ourselves in the way the Father and the Son govern themselves in and with the world.

Promise Is the Foundation for Forgiveness and Repentance

The kinship between forgiveness and promise is displayed by the etymology of the words themselves. As we discussed earlier, "promise" comes from a Latin root meaning "to send forth." This is similar to the Old English root meaning "to give forth" from which the English word "forgive" is derived. The Greek word for "forgive" has a similar meaning; it is a compound of two words meaning "to send from." These similarities are no mere coincidence, but reveal the intimate connection between promise and forgiveness.

The seminal truth is that promise and forgiveness are reciprocal. Promise is sending ourselves forth to another; forgiveness is releasing another from the debt we believe they owe us. Promise binds us, forgiveness releases others and ourselves as well. Promise is the way God has ordained us to be bound to one another. The counterfeit binding is the revenge of unforgiveness. Whenever we do not forgive others, we are bound to the one who hurt or betrayed us.

Think of the worst violation you can imagine—perhaps being raped or molested by a relative for example. This is an unspeakable betrayal. Paradoxically, without forgiveness, without releasing the person from our desire for revenge, we will remain bound to the very ones who have hurt us. Francis Frangipane defines bitterness as "unfulfilled revenge."[18] The

---

[18]Francis Frangipane, *The Three Battlegrounds*, 50.

longer we refuse to forgive those who hurt us the more unforgiveness hardens into bitterness. The transformation is inevitable.

One of the mysteries of God is that He respects our choices. The creator of the universe restrains Himself based on our choices. The practice of forgiveness releases these unholy bonds and restores us to the freedom of being bound by promise alone. Jesus said, "I tell you the truth, whatever you bind on earth will be bound in heaven, and whatever you loose on earth will be loosed in heaven (Matthew 18:18, NIV). When we forgive another, God forgives us and gives us the grace to repent. When we hold bitterness and judgment toward another, we reap God's judgment, for "by your standard of measure, it will be measured to you" (Luke 6:38).

I (Derek) know a man who filed for divorce from his wife because of many disappointments in their marriage, including her chronic addiction to alcohol. After his divorce, he refused to become intimate with anyone else for fear of the same disappointments. His unforgiveness became bitterness toward all women. Ironically, his harsh judgement of his wife and resulting bitterness led him into the very sin he condemned her for—raging alcoholism.

This dynamic is inescapable in the universe. It is an expression of God's principle of sowing and reaping (Galatians 6:7). Throughout our lives, we continually sow and reap, bind and loose. We must release ourselves and others from our unforgiveness and bitterness before we are totally free to bind ourselves to them in promise.

The Lord's prayer reads, "forgive us our debts as we forgive our debtors." These debtors are "those who fail in their duty toward us."[19] Duties, which are obligations to others, result from explicit and implicit promises. A promise sets up the target—the bulls-eye at which we are shooting. As Christians our target is always to love others with the same commitment God demonstrates toward us in keeping His promises. When people miss the mark with us, we release them through forgiveness from the duty of the specific promises they made to us. This release or 'giving forth' of forgiveness frees the other person to rededicate himself in promise to us if he chooses.   Without forgiveness, both of us would be bound—the maker of the promise in self-righteousness and the receiver in bitterness.

Duties are the province of justice. Thomas Aquinas defined justice as "a habit whereby a man renders to each one his due with constant and perpetual will."[20] Justice depends on promise, because justice deals with rights and duties. Promise is the source of all rights and duties, even natural or so-called inalienable rights. Joseph Pieper, an expert on Aquinas, wrote,

That something belongs to man inalienably means this: the man who does not give a person what belongs to him, withholds it or deprives him of it, is really doing harm to himself;   he   is   the   one   who   actually   loses something—indeed, in the most extreme case, he even destroys himself. At all events, something incomparably worse befalls him than happens to the one who suffers an injustice: that is how inviolable the right is![21]

---

[19]Spiros Zodhiates, *The Complete Word Study Dictionary of the New Testament*, 1079.

[20]Josef Pieper, *The Four Cardinal Virtues*, 44.

[21]*The Four Cardinal Virtues*, 47.

Promise transforms rights into duties. When we are concerned with our rights, our focus is on ourselves. When, on the other hand, our will is directed to others, our duties to them fill our consciousness. Only a master is occupied by rights; a servant is concerned with duties and what he owes others. In God's economy, the one who knows his duties and forgets his rights is the greatest of all: "And sitting down, [Jesus] called the twelve and said to them, 'If anyone wants to be first, he shall be last of all, and servant of all'" (Mark 9:35). A servant never asserts his rights in relationship to others.

The New Testament says we are to forgive not only sins but debts, evil speaking, transgressions, and iniquities. All of these can be divided into two groups: each of them deal with the external, visible act, except for iniquity, which is an internal state. Iniquity means "lawlessness." It points to an attitude of the heart that leads to the specific external acts—the sin, debts, speaking ill of another (slander), and transgressions. Each of these acts is a different physical manifestation of the internal iniquity of the heart.

Each of these acts produces a disruption in your relationship with God and others. Forgiveness releases the other person from the guilt of causing the disruption. Forgiveness takes place between people. It must be walked out. Every time a sin, offense, or slander binds us to another, forgiveness is what releases us. Forgiveness is a continual surrendering of the many violations of our rights and a continual giving forth of oneself to relationship *in spite of* the injury sustained at the hands of the other.

The Scriptures say that we "are being transformed into the same image [i.e., His image] from glory to glory, just as from the Lord, the Spirit" (II Corinthians 3:18). "Glory," according to *Webster's Third New International Dictionary,* "is the lofty praise, honor, or admiration extended by common consent." This is a mystery, but Scripture reveals that what we endure here on earth—the hardships, the difficulties, whatever we suffer—are "producing for us an eternal weight of glory far beyond all comparison" (II Corinthians 4:17). God's heart toward us is full of praise, honor, and admiration when we keep our promises. The crowning glory of kept promises will be His invitation to "enter . . . into My rest, thou good and faithful servant." The path from glory to glory is our faithfulness in keeping promises. Each kept promise opens up possibilities for other promises, and even greater glory. This progression involves both our faith and our conscience.

Faith is strengthened by keeping promises. Jesus said, "He who is faithful in a very little thing is faithful also in much" (Luke 16:10). As we keep the small promises we make—being on time, being honest, doing what we say we will do—we become fully persuaded that we are capable of doing that and much more. Jesus promises us that "he who believes in Me, the works that I do shall he do also; and greater works than these shall he do; because I go to the Father" (John 14:12). Accomplishing the greatest deeds starts with keeping the smallest promises.

In keeping promises, we not only strengthen our faith, but we also educate our consciences. As we become aware of the promises we make—those we keep, and those we don't—our conscience comes awake and alert. When our conscience is numb, which Scripture calls a "seared conscience" (I Timothy 4:2), we do not even perceive the possibilities for relationships with those around us. In our numbness, we settle for bland, unrewarding relationships. In the great game of life, we begin playing not to lose rather than playing to win. We give up on our relationships with our spouses, with our children, with our friends and begin to hope to just get by. Like the servant who takes the talent and buries it in order not to risk losing it, the precious relationships in our lives become stagnant and lose their vibrancy. To waken the conscience from its slumber is an uncomfortable process, much like awakening your foot when it falls asleep. To waken the conscience requires us to be aware of others and the difference we make with them.

In accounting for our broken promises, we get to experience the pain we cause others. The righteous sorrow that we feel for others compels us to transformation; it is the godly sorrow that leads to repentance. As we begin to wake up to their lives, we cross over into a deeper sense of the purpose and meaning of our existence. The compassion we experience destroys the myth of our own worthlessness.

God does not want our relationships to become stagnant, or our relationship with Him to die from neglect. His plan is for increasing love, increasing intimacy, and a never-ending increase of joy in fellowship with each other and with Him. The path to an ever-increasing relationship with God and each other is that of promise, the path that Jesus Himself took.

Each promise we keep gives glory to the Promise of the ages, who is Jesus Christ. Each kept promise recalls the promise that Jesus kept to reconcile all things in heaven and earth to God. Each redeemed broken promise shows His forgiveness and grace. Even when someone to whom we've broken a promise does not forgive us, we can demonstrate the grace and forgiveness of the Lord by loving him anyway.

Nothing else in our life comes as close to the heart of God as keeping a promise.

Promise is the heart of reconciliation, worship, and prayer

Through making and keeping promises, we participate in the purpose that Jesus came to accomplish: reconciling others to God vertically and to each other horizontally. With the most awesome and surprising command, Jesus asks us to step into His shoes with one another. He says to "Love one another as I have loved you, so you must love one another" (John 13:34).

In the New Testament, two Greek words are both translated as the English verb "to reconcile." Both words have similar meanings: "to set up a relationship of peace not existing before" and "to restore a relationship of peace that has been disturbed."

Love's pleasure is to ransom itself for the beloved. In order to establish peace in our relationship with God, He sent His only, unique Son to stand in our place and suffer the punishment that was rightfully ours. This act demonstrates what it is to be a ransom, which Webster defines as "the price paid to free a prisoner from captivity or punishment." Paul describes this process of reconciliation in Ephesians:

> Therefore, remember that formerly you who are Gentiles by birth and called "uncircumcised" by those who call themselves "the circumcision" (that done in the body by the hands of men)—remember that at that time you were separate from Christ, excluded from citizenship in Israel and foreigners to the covenants of the promise, without hope and without God in the world. But now in Christ Jesus you who once were far away have been brought near through the blood of Christ. For he himself is our peace, who has made the two one and has destroyed the barrier, the dividing wall of hostility, by abolishing in his flesh the law with its commandments and regulations. His purpose was

to create in himself one new man out of the two, thus making peace, and in this one body to reconcile both of them to God through the cross, by which he put to death their hostility. He came and preached peace to you who were far away and peace to those who were near. For through him we both have access to the Father by one Spirit. (Ephesians 2:11-18, NIV)

It is through Jesus' sacrifice that the "covenants of promise" were made available to us—those to whom the original promise was not made. Just as we can be reconciled to God vertically through being grafted into the covenants of promise, promise also is the heart of reconciliation horizontally between our neighbors and ourselves. The "sending forth" that results in reconciliation is the sending forth of ourselves as ransoms: the price or provision that reestablishes relationship.

Just as Jesus sent himself forth as a ransom—paying the price that reestablished our relationship with God if we believe—we can likewise establish peace in our relationships with others. But only if we are willing to pay the price.

Often, our urge to be right keeps us from paying the price to reconcile with our spouses, friends, and neighbors. I (Derek) remember a disagreement I had with a friend in college. I don't recall the specifics of the disagreement, other than my absolute certainty that I was *right*. I was so determined to be right that my friend withdrew from me. Oh, we spoke, but only about surface issues. We lost the intimacy we had enjoyed before. Even at that young age, I knew our relationship was disturbed. And so it remained until I was willing to value my friend above being right. Just as Jesus sent Himself to the disciples and the whole world in humility, laying aside his "equality with God" (which was rightfully due

Him) and becoming a servant; so too, He commands us to lay aside being right and give ourselves to our neighbors through our promises.

The peace that is established in reconciliation between men is unilateral. Regardless of the external circumstances, we can be at peace. Our peace is not contingent; it does not depend on anything or anyone other than our relationship with Jesus. Zodhiates defines it this way:

> Peace is the tranquil state of a soul assured of its salvation through Christ, fearing nothing from God and consequently content with its earthly lot, whatever it is. This is the direct result of redemption by Christ and consists primarily of a state of conscious reconciliation with God, although it is often used in a broader sense to denote all the blessings which accompany and flow from that reconciliation.[22]

My subjective awareness of peace is a moment-to-moment indication of how I am relating to God. If I am trusting Him as my provision regardless of the circumstances, I experience peace. Peace is the evidence of the kingdom of God within. Throughout the centuries, this peace has enabled disciples of Jesus to persevere through torture, crucifixion, and the worst of horrors. Not only does peace signal the kingdom within, but the lack of peace indicates an interruption in our life with God. The lack of peace also reveals an idol. Rather than depending on God, we are looking to someone or something else to provide for us.

---

[22] Spiros Zodhiates, *The Complete Word Study Dictionary: New Testament*, 520.

Peace is distinct from apathy. Stoic indifference and apathy are not peace; they are counterfeit peace. Being concerned with the self, they are opposed to the peace of God. The peace from God is not about self but about Him and who He is, the relationship that we as believers have with Him, and the position that He has placed us in. Apathy says "I am nothing, I don't matter, I don't make a difference anyway." Peace says, "The God of the Universe loves me and knows me; my life is in His hands; He is the author and finisher of my whole life and faith. Therefore, He will use me for His purpose of glorifying Himself by blessing others through me."

The peace that God brings also frees us to view every circumstance as God's provision. We are tempted to label situations, circumstances, and other forms of feedback in our lives as "good" or "bad," when in reality they are neither good nor bad. Feedback is just information. But if we continuously label feedback as "bad," we will not view it as something sent from God to finish my faith.

I (Derek) know a man who is in his early forties, who has spent most of his business life in sales. Even though he consistently meets or exceeds his sales quotas, he has never held down any one job for more than three years. He never sees his firings as feedback, but inevitably lays the blame on an attack from Satan. I think it has more to do with how he relates to people, but because he attributes his results to an attack from the enemy, he never sees his own need to change. As a matter of fact, if anything, he uses Satan to enable himself to continue being with people in ways that are ineffective. Having the peace of God frees us to account for our actions based on the feedback of the physical universe. God's peace comes whenever we know that our identity is secure in God—nothing on earth or in heaven can threaten who we are. We are thus freed to love others and desire the best for them, which means keeping our promises regardless of the cost.

The freedom to account for actions and promises allows us to be flexible. Rather than defending my position or action, I can see if it accomplished what I intended. When my actions and promises do not accomplish my intent, I can shift to something else.

Just as our promise is at the heart of reconciliation, so it is for worship. Worship is an attitude of laying oneself before another in order to show respect or to make a supplication; usually worship is given to someone of superior rank. The worship we now give to God is just a shadow of the worship we will give Him when we see Him face-to-face.

Today, through the glass darkly, we only see Jesus' holiness as it relates to us. We interpret who Jesus is through our own experience. But to be holy means to be set apart or to be wholly other. Donald W. McCullough expresses how totally separate and different Jesus is:

> . . . [H]oliness blazes into fulfillment in Jesus Christ—the One through whom God reveals a separateness precisely in a gracious commitment *not* to be separate, the One through whom the otherness of God becomes a conflagration against sin, but with flames that ignite an incandescence of truth in our darkness, that warm our lonely coldness, that kindle a fire of love in our own hearts. The saving grace of God in Jesus Christ sets a clear boundary between God and humanity; it moves along a one-way street, coming from God and accomplished in the power of God, as it judges the world's sin. And yet this judgment draws an inclusive boundary around a new relationship between God and humanity; . . . it destroys the alienating power of sin by nailing it to the cross and opens the door to new life through the empty tomb. The holiness of God—wholly

other as it is wholly *for*— separates and unites, judges and saves.[23]

McCollough is describing the characteristics of promise in this passage. One unequivocal difference that makes Jesus wholly other than us is He never failed to keep His promises; every last one. In keeping promises, we worship Jesus, the fulfillment of all of God's promises. As Psalm 50 says:

Do you think I feast on venison? Or drink draughts of goats' blood? Spread for me a banquet of praise, serve High God a feast of kept promises, and call for help when you are in trouble—I'll help you, and you'll honor me."[24]

We worship God by treating others the way God treats them.

In the Lord's prayer, Jesus taught us first of all to bring honor to His name. We honor God's name by promise. Second, He taught us to pray for God's kingdom to come. We also bring in the kingdom through promise. The coming of the kingdom depends wholly on promise—without the sending forth of the Son into the world, the kingdom would not have come to the earth. In the Lord's prayer, as in all prayer, promise is the backdrop. Specifically, prayer relies on the promise that if we ask, seek, and knock, God will hear and answer our prayers. Then we are to pray for His kingdom to come on earth as it is in heaven.

In the Great Commission, Jesus sends us forth to expand the kingdom:

---

[23]Donald W. McCullough, *Trivializing God*, 81-82.

[24]Eugene H. Peterson, *Psalms*, 73.

And Jesus came up and spoke to them, saying, "All authority has been given to Me in heaven and on earth. Go therefore and make disciples of all the nations, baptizing them in the name of the Father and the Son and the Holy Spirit, teaching them to observe all that I commanded you; and lo, I am with you always, even to the end of the age" (Matthew 28:18-20).

He ends by giving us the promise of His presence and with His presence, all authority in heaven and on earth. He promises us the provision of everything pertaining to life and godliness (II Peter 1:3).

As the church has been overcome with the existentialism of our culture, we have come to believe that the love we feel in our hearts toward God has an independent reality. We think that we can love God even when our relationships are discordant, strident, and full of enmity toward others. Perhaps even worse, we believe that we love God when we are indifferent to others. Promise interrupts the isolation of subjective emotion and directs us to reach another. The first epistle of John hits the heart of this issue:

"If someone says, 'I love God,' and hates his brother, he is a liar; for the one who does not love his brother whom he has seen, cannot love God whom he has not seen" (I John 4:20).

"I don't *hate* my brother," you may well interject—but the absence of hate, if it is not filled with love, is indifference. This is the worst hatred of all. The horror of the Nazis was not just the slaughter of six million Jews in the Holocaust, but the complete indifference with which they acted. The Nuremberg trials shocked the world by revealing the Nazis' attitude that the Jews were just animals and thus not worthy of remorse.

How different are we than the Nazis? If we are indifferent to others—indifferent to the promises they make to us and we to them—our love for God, even if it burns within us, is useless. If we love others as shown through keeping promises, we love God; if we are indifferent to others and the promises we have made them, we are indifferent to God.

Our attitude toward the promises we make reveals the stance of our hearts toward God. Promise provides a window on our hearts and clears away the fog of our own bias. The only place that we can reach God, the only place that He has promised to be found in the world is in the hearts of men.

C. S. Lewis encourages us to consider the weight of glory that each person we meet, however homely or humble, may carry in God's kingdom:

> It may be possible for each to think too much of his own potential glory hereafter; it is hardly possible for him to think too often or too deeply about that of his neighbor. The load, or weight, or burden of my neighbor's glory should be laid daily on my back, a load so heavy that only humility can carry it, and the backs of the proud will be broken. It is a serious thing to live in a society of possible gods and goddesses, to remember that the dullest and most uninteresting person you talk to may one day be a creature which, if you saw it now, you would be strongly tempted to worship, or else a horror and a corruption such as you now meet, if at all, only in a nightmare. All day long we are, in some degree, helping each other to one or other of these destinations. It is in the light of these overwhelming possibilities, it is with the awe and the circumspection proper to them, that we should conduct all our dealings with one another, all friendships, all loves, all play, all

politics. There are no ordinary people. You have never talked to a mere mortal.[25]

The weight of glory for each of us is built upon the foundation of our relationship with God. Each promise kept to our brothers and sisters adds to the glory carried in God's heart toward us. Laying up treasure in heaven is not just a metaphor—it describes the reality of the power of kept promises.

---

[25]C.S. Lewis, *The Weight of Glory*, 18-19.

6. Idolatry—The Victim's Way of Relating

Dear children, keep yourselves from idols.

I John 5:21 (NIV)

Victims are idolaters. Every victim sets up some idol, whether it is an idol of appearance, image, or form, which he then worships. This is a blunt statement, but as we shall see, this reflects exactly the nature of being a victim.

Take appearances. I (Dan) saw how strongly I value my appearance during an important dinner with friends and ministry supporters. I wanted to speak with someone, let's call him Mark, about making a substantial donation to Mashiyach Ministries. While we were waiting for our entrees, I filled him in on my background and history. I warmed to my subject—after all, it's one of my favorites! Suddenly, I found myself exaggerating an experience I had overseas. Before I knew it, I implied that I'd been centrally involved in documented miracles when, in reality, I had only visited the site after the miracles had occurred. As I looked into Mark's eyes, I was filled with a sense of dread—my conscience fired off a huge warning shot. I lost my train of thought and began to perspire profusely; I excused myself to go to the men's room.

I looked in the mirror. My face was ashen and I felt trapped. I knew that the implication of my story was a lie; but I certainly did not want to tell anyone! I begged and pleaded with God. Surely there must be some way out of this predicament that would preserve how I looked with my friends. I raced through a number of alternative deals I could make with God—not saying anything about my lie, but refraining from requesting the donation; talking about some of my other problems and sins in order to balance their opinion of me, but still ask for the money; complain of sudden stomach pain and leave immediately. My conscience would not relent however. Each of these "deals" was a further lie. Nothing would redeem this situation but the truth. I knew that I had to confess my sin.

When I returned to the table, the entrees had been served, and again I was tempted to avoid my confession. The conversation had moved on to other, lighter topics. Why ruin dinner for everyone? Stuffing my pride and terror of revealing my lack of integrity, I sat down and said, "I have something to confess." The table fell silent as all eyes turned quizzically to me.

"I lied. I wasn't involved in those miracles like I implied; I only visited afterward." I stopped and waited while my words sank in. This had been easier than I thought!

Mark was the first to speak: "Why did you lie?" My sense of relief evaporated, leaving an empty pit in my stomach; I started sweating again.

"I wanted to impress you. I wanted your financial support too. I didn't believe that my background was enough. I wanted to look more spiritual, more powerful, and ultimately, I guess, more worthy of a donation."

As I accounted for my sin and we discussed what was behind it, Mark and I were drawn into a more intimate relationship with each other. He identified with my temptation and decided right there to make a gift to our organization because of my honesty in owning up to my lie.

Images are similar to appearances, but of longer duration. An appearance is instantaneous. An image, on the other hand, is built up over weeks, months, and even years. Our image is the outward persona that we consistently project to those around us—the powerful business man, the submissive wife, the stylish model, the rebellious teenager, the artistic maverick, the hippy professor, the good student, and so on. These images are powerful societal icons ingrained in us in childhood, and usually carry hidden messages: "big boys don't cry (be a man)," "get a hold of yourself (your emotions bother me)," "nobody likes a cry baby (don't rock the boat)," "nails that stick out get pounded down (behave appropriately)." These societal and family myths are handed down from father to son, from mother to daughter, on the playground, in the classroom, at church. We embed these truths deep within our identities. They become part of our self-images—which then are reinforced over and over through advertising, television, and the movies.

Through years of training, one of my (Derek's) carefully constructed images was that of always being rational and in control. When the image was recently threatened while watching a sentimental movie, I did everything in my power to keep the façade in place. I was watching the movie *Sand Lot* with Laurie and my sons. The movie is about a group of "athletically-challenged" boys who love to play sand lot baseball. Because of their lack of athletic prowess, the boys resort to playing among themselves until a very gifted player decides to join them and coach them. One scene, which was not particularly poignant to anyone else, hit me right in the gut. Sadness overwhelmed me with a sudden urge to break out in wracking sobs. I managed to clamp down on these "unmanly" emotions and keep these feelings to myself. Rather than losing control, I didn't even shed a tear.

Even on the way home, the tears remained close to the surface. I mentioned to Laurie that I found that scene to be very emotional, but refused to talk about if for fear I would break loose.

For days, I wondered what those intense feelings were about and why I had not released them by crying. I finally realized that I valued *understanding* my emotions above *expressing* them. My image of myself as a rational adult meant more to me than expressing my honest emotion. Rationality was, at that moment, the idol I worshiped.

I even came to understand *why* I felt so strongly, which is much different than feeling the strength of emotion itself. It had to do with starting little league baseball as a fourth-grader with my dad's 1940's vintage baseball glove. The other boys laughed at me and I *still* carried that feeling of exposure and ridicule with me. As the audience laughed at the players on the screen, a deep well of pain revealed itself in me and threatened to come rushing out. Rather than seeing this as God's provision for healing that deep hurt, I tried to bury it even deeper, so that I could maintain my image of rationality even with the people closest to me!

Whereas images and appearances center on how we look and relate to those around us, form is an idol dedicated to the way things are done. While I (Larry) was preparing to become a trainer for Mashiyach, I attended a mock training session where we practiced on each other. I was introducing one of the experiential exercises in the *Momentus* training. As I stood up and looked into the eyes of the small group of "participants," I became anxious and self-conscious. I began stumbling over my words. I was shocked! For years I had regularly preached to gatherings of up to several thousand people. But in a room with only thirteen people, I was freezing up. After stumbling through my first attempt, I tried again. I started off a little better, but began to fall back into the self-consciousness that had doomed my first try. In frustration, I cried out, "I can see what I am doing, I can see what I'm doing!" One of the participants called out, "That's the problem Larry, you can see what *you* are doing." In other words, I made an idol out of the form; then I tried to look good by following the form. While I was spending so much time and energy attempting to look good, others experienced me as suspicious and guarded—waiting to be revealed as a fraud like the Wizard of Oz behind the curtain. How on earth was I ever going to help anyone if all I cared about was myself?

We see the idol of form whenever someone slavishly asserts that a certain thing can only be done one way. Most of us know the old story of the young bride making her first Christmas ham. She carefully cut the ends off the ham before putting it into the roasting pan. Curious, her husband asked her why she did this. She didn't know. Her mother had always done it that way. The husband would not be so quickly put off, so he called his mother-in-law. Her answer was nearly identical: she did not know, other than *her* mother had always cut the ends off the ham. Finally, they called the young bride's grandmother in the nursing home. The answer was quite simple: the grandmother always cut the ham in half because it would not fit into her small roasting pan! So it is with the idol of form, the original reason for adopting the form gets lost or becomes obsolete, but the form lives on and gains strength with age.

Concepts and principles can become idols just as can a particular form. These favored doctrines and principles are held as fundamental truths. We sacrifice many relationships on the altar of these convictions. From the workaholic who never spends time with his family in order to "provide a good living"—until his wife files divorce in frustration—to the husband whose pride will not allow his wife to work even though his family is teetering on poverty, we turn convictions into idols. They no longer aid us in serving others. Rather, our convictions often keep us from others, because we serve the idols.

Whether it is providing a superior living standard or being the sole breadwinner so your spouse can stay at home with the kids, these convictions or beliefs form the basis and structure of our world view. For example, many churches believe that people can't handle pain, even if it might ultimately lead to healing and deliverance. Consequently, they censor honest communication that might lead to pain. Families train children with the wornout axiom, "if you don't have anything nice to say, don't say anything at all."

We worship each of these idols—appearances, images, forms and convictions—in the American church, the family, and society. We do not worship by bowing down or offering burnt sacrifices or singing songs of praise. Our worship is much more subtle. It is revealed in the presuppositions we carry with us. We prejudge what we will value and what we will not; what is worth our time, energy and money, and what is not. Idolatry is a value system, in which we decide that something else is worthy of greater devotion than the Lord.

Whatever we worship reveals what is *most* important to us in that moment. For me (Derek) at the movie theater, it was important to be rational and in control of my emotions; the classic image of a man—tough, in control, and untouchable. I valued this image more than sharing that moment of pain with my wife and sons.

When those intense feelings began to surface, I did not consciously choose between my image and authenticity. It was as if I didn't choose my response, but it chose me. This is the nature of all idolatry: we first choose our idols, and then our idols choose us.

This happens subtly—over the years we forget the original choices we made that led us into idolatry. The path to killing the victim and destroying the idols that hold us begins with remembering. For me (Dan), the incident at the restaurant with my friend, Mark, inspired me to dig deeply into my past to uncover the roots of the idol.

I first had to identify the idol. As I talked with Mark after dinner, I recognized the idol as one of appearances. I desperately needed to appear spiritually powerful and special in my relationship with God. But why? Why would I jeopardize a valued friendship by lying? As I looked deeper, I began to realize I had surrendered my freedom to the idol as a child. It controlled me in situations where I feared that my performance would not be enough to gain God's provision or man's approval. As a result, my love for others was conditional and I did not trust God to provide for me and my family.

In discovering the nature of this idol in my life, I was able to connect it to judgments I had made about my father when I was growing up. My dad constantly compared me to another athlete in town and ribbed me whenever he outperformed me. I judged my father's love as conditional and something I could only win by my performance. I hated him, based on that belief. Even though my judgment of my dad was not true—he loved *me* not just my performance—I acted *as if* it were. I still longed for his approval so I began exaggerating to make myself bigger in his eyes and the eyes of others (so I thought). My bitterness toward my dad and the exaggerations I used to cover it infected all my relationships as a young man. Many friends only believed half of what I said.

By the time I was 14, my exaggerations and lies had become so pervasive in my relationship with my father that he no longer trusted me. I did not address this issue with him until my addiction recovery process. Only then did I begin to work through many issues of unforgiveness with my father, mother, and God. Now, *years* later, the idol still ambushed me at dinner with my friend. I felt like a victim; the choice to lie through exaggeration had been made and forgotten years before. And yet it still had power over me in times of insecurity.

The on-going identification of these idols calls me to repent from my need to look good by performing well, and my need of men's approval. Each time that I face up, confess and repent for my actions and thoughts, and reveal the idol, I find a greater freedom the next time I am in a similar situation. This liberation produces an intimacy and support with my parents, family, and friends that I never thought possible, not to mention a trust with others that I did not have before my recovery.

Hosea wrote, "They set up kings without my consent; they choose princes without my approval. With their silver and gold they make idols for themselves to their own destruction" (Hosea 8:4). When he says, "they set up kings without my consent; they choose princes without my approval," he reveals the truth that we choose our own idols, which then become so comfortable to us we barely know that they are still there. In choosing the kings and princes—the idols—of our lives, we begin to let them define who we are. Our idols dictate who we are, how we act, where we go, and with whom.

Who Are You?

Suppose someone asks you, "Who are you?" What is your response? Take a moment with this question. Most often, it evokes a list of descriptive words about what we do or have done, how we are related to others, the roles in which we serve, and so on. Answers such as: I am an evangelical Christian, I am an atheist, I am a housewife, I am a college graduate, I am an alcoholic, I am a lawyer, a doctor, an Indian chief, a minister, and so forth.

Contrast these answers with the answer God gave to this same question. When God appeared to Moses in the burning bush and commissioned him to go to Pharaoh and demand the release of God's people, Moses asked God this same question:

> Then Moses said to God, "Behold, I am going to the sons of Israel, and I shall say to them, 'The God of your fathers has sent me to you.' Now they may say to me, 'What is His name?' What shall I say to them?" And God said to Moses, "I AM WHO I AM"; and He said, "Thus you shall say to the sons of Israel, 'I AM has sent me to you.'" (Exodus 3:13-14)

Answering the question, "who are you?" with a list of descriptive terms is a subtle manifestation of idolatry. Our identities in no way depend on our performance or position. We are who God made us to be. God could have responded to Moses with a list of descriptive words about Himself: I am the Creator of the Universe, the Eternal Living God, the Consuming Fire, Mighty One of Israel, Everlasting God, El Shaddai (God Almighty), Branch of Righteousness, the Lord our righteousness, Shepherd, Servant, Word of God—all of which are true. However, describing His identity—who He is—with a list of descriptive terms, limits Him. By saying "I AM WHO I AM," He does not limit Himself. When we talk *about* God, using human terms and analogies, we limit Him and reduce Him to a metaphor and an idol. But when we turn to Him and address Him directly, we do not fall into this idolatry. Martin Buber described this reality beautifully:

> The eternal *Thou* can by its nature not become *It*; for by its nature it cannot be established in measure and bounds, not even in the measure of the immeasurable, or the bounds of

boundless being; for by its nature it cannot be understood as a sum of qualities, not even as an infinite sum of qualities raised to a transcendental level; for it can be found neither in nor out of the world; for it cannot be experienced, or thought for we miss Him, Him who is, if we say "I believe that He is"—"He" is also a metaphor, but *"Thou"* is not.[26]

As with God, so with us. We do not have the privilege of claiming the self-existent nature of the Creator which is implicit in "I AM WHO I AM." At best we can declare, "I am whom He created." Notice the categories with which you define yourself. These are the areas in which you may have created idolatrous relationships. They reflect your circumstances, your relationship to those around you, and the roles you serve.

Each idol we choose to worship steals a measure of our freedom. If someone values his image, would he be free to go to the grocery store or mall with greasy hair? If the idols were physical comfort and ease would the person endure difficulty and pain for much of anything or anyone?

Idolatry and being a victim go hand in hand. One is not possible without the other. Just as promise expresses the love of God, idolatry expresses the nature of Satan and Antichrist. Idolatry is the express nature of Satan and the source of all sin, because when we indulge in idolatry, we put something else in the position that only God rightfully fills in our life. Herbert Schlossberg defined idolatry as:

> any substitution of what is created for the creator. People may worship nature, money, mankind, power, history, or

[26]Martin Buber, *I and Thou*, 112.

social and political systems instead of the God who created them all.[27]

There is only one Creator. Every time we relate to something else as if that something defines us, it is an instance of idolatry.

The conflict between worshiping the creature and worshiping the Creator began when Satan turned from worshiping God to worshiping himself. This same battle rages in the human heart. As Paul wrote to the Galatians, "For the sinful nature desires what is contrary to the Spirit, and the Spirit what is contrary to the sinful nature. They are in conflict with each other, so that you do not do what you want." (Galatians 5:17, NIV). In the battleground of the human heart, this fight continues.

When I (Dan) was a young boy I went to weekly catechism classes at the local Catholic church. At catechism, I read accounts from the Bible in which Jesus responded with love and compassion to questions challenging His authority, purpose, and identity. Two scriptures intrigued me. The first was the command to "love God with all our heart, soul, strength and mind and our neighbor as ourselves" (Luke 10:27) and the second was the proverb "Iron sharpens iron, so one man sharpens another" (Proverbs 27:17).

At the same time, a nun threatened to expel an acquaintance of mine from the class for believing and dressing differently than the rest of us. My friend, let's call her Theresa, refused to wear a skirt. Wearing pants was not technically a violation of any rule, but Theresa was something of a firebrand in class. She questioned nearly every belief that the Sister held dear—the use of the rosary, prayers to saints, the authority of the Pope, the use of the liturgy. The threat of expulsion arose

---

[27]Herbert Schlossberg, *Idols for Destruction*, 6.

one afternoon because Theresa was wearing wool slacks and a blouse. The Sister said she had to go home and change into a skirt. Theresa asked why. The nun told her that she had to submit because of the authority of the church. In the course of the argument, Theresa questioned the infallibility of the Pope. The Sister became incensed and demanded that Theresa retract her statements and questions about the Pope. If she did not, she would be expelled permanently. She then sent Theresa to the priest's office.

After she left, the Sister told the rest of us not to associate with Theresa, or we too would be expelled.

I was terrified. Although I did not agree with what Theresa believed, I still wanted to explore what she was saying. However, I did not want to be expelled from class in the process! I believed even then that the only way to know the truth is to test it pragmatically in debate and practice. I was confused by the Sister's fear of Theresa's beliefs. I thought, "Why would the Sister be so afraid of Theresa's behavior and beliefs, if what the Sister believed was the truth? Why wouldn't she simply want to convince Theresa of the truth?"

When I spoke to the nun privately about my thoughts and concerns, she immediately sent me to the priest. During our interview, he asked me what I believed in the matter. "Why is that important?" I asked. He said that in order to be Catholic I had to believe the right doctrine and that I must follow it in unconditional obedience.

"Who made this up?" I asked. He said the Pope had decided it and therefore I must believe it as if God Himself had spoken it. I stewed over this for months. Something was not right. When I began to consider Jesus' command to love God with all my heart, soul, strength and mind and my neighbor as myself, I began to understand that my love for God was different than my love for my neighbor, even the Pope. As a Christian I was commanded to love my neighbor, to love the whole race, all men, even my enemy, and to make no exception, either of partiality or of dislike. Loving in this way is not possible without God's help. Only Jesus could love this way.

The only one I am commanded to love unconditionally is God. This commandment does not say to love God as I love myself. *To love another man with all my heart, soul, strength and mind or to permit someone to love me in that way is idolatrous.* Yet the priest was telling me to give unconditional obedience to another man.

As I came to understand the difference between loving God and loving my neighbor, I was profoundly convicted of the ramifications implied in the promise to love another as myself: I could no longer be silent or indifferent when I believed that something a friend was doing was harmful to him. Years later I read this quote in the *Works of Love* by Søren Kierkegaard:

> If your beloved or friend asks something of you that you, precisely because you honestly loved, had in concern considered would be harmful to him, then you must bear a responsibility if you love by obeying instead of loving by refusing a fulfillment of the desire. But you shall love God in unconditional obedience, even if what he requires of you might seem to you to be to your own harm, indeed, harmful to his cause; for God's wisdom is beyond all comparison with yours, and God's governance has no obligation of responsibility in relation to your sagacity. All you have to do is to obey in love. A human being, however, you shall only —but, no, this is indeed the highest—a human being you shall love as yourself. If you can perceive what is best for him better than he can, you will not be excused because the harmful thing was his own desire, was what he himself asked for. If this were not the case, it would be quite proper to speak of loving another person more than oneself,

because this would mean, despite one's insight that this would be harmful to him, doing it *in obedience* because he demanded it, or *in adoration* because he desire it. But you expressly have no right to do this; you have the responsibility if you do it, just as the other has the responsbility if he wants to misuse his relation to you in such a way.[28]

This statement, found years later, confirmed my desire in Catechism to love my neighbor as myself.

Demanding unconditional obedience to a man fosters idolatry, but is not confined to those in the Catholic church. It is rampant in the Evangelical Church, in corporate America, and between husbands and wives, as well. Daily we tempt and sometimes even demand others to give us and our organizations the love, loyalty, and unconditional obedience they owe only to God.

What sickens me even today about this whole childhood episode with the Catholic Church is the coercion exerted by both the nun and the priest. This coercion is rooted in idolatry—the idea that the Church can dictate that I should honor a man in blind obedience goes against every promise and commandment of God. It is worshiping the creature not the creator.

How often this kind of idolatry slips by us! Could it be that we rarely see the extent of the idolatry in our lives? We live in a titanic battle between the forces of God and the forces of idolatry—that battle swirls around the promises we make.

---

[28]Søren Kierkegaard, *Works of Love*, 19-20.

The Battle Rages

This battle between promise and idolatry has raged in every human heart from the Garden of Eden onward. Promise, as we have seen, is God's hallmark. Whenever I choose to live my word for another person, I make myself a servant rather than the master.

God is a jealous God and brooks no competitors on the throne. God staked out His territory explicitly in the Ten Commandments:

> You shall have no other gods before Me. You shall not make for yourself an idol, or any likeness of what is in heaven above or on the earth beneath or in the water under the earth. You shall not worship them or serve them; for I, the LORD your God, am a jealous God, visiting the iniquity of the fathers on the children, on the third and the fourth generations of those who hate Me (Exodus 20:3-5).

The Lord is unequivocal: to place an idol before Him is to *hate* Him.

As the battle becomes fiercer at the end of the age, we must be prepared to uproot the idolatry in our hearts. To be effective against idolatry, we must draw the battle lines clearly and know the Enemy and his patterns. The Enemy of our souls is Satan. Satan's impact on our lives—his fingerprint—is death. Scripture also says that "The last enemy that will be abolished is death" (I Corinthians 15:26). The tool Satan uses to bring death is sin ("the wages of sin is death," Romans 6:23). The source of sin is idolatry. We must be able to trace whatever brings death in our relationships and our lives back to the source; we must find the idol and dethrone it.

Our language predisposes us to think that idolatry depends on the idol; that idolatry is worshiping certain objects but never other ones. This is not true. We can make anyone and anything into an idol by how we relate to that person or thing. The Apostle Paul plainly wrote that objects are not in themselves idols:

> We know that an idol is nothing at all in the world and that there is no God but one. For even if there are so-called gods, whether in heaven or on earth (as indeed there are many "gods" and many "lords"), yet for us there is but one God, the Father, from whom all things came and for whom we live; and there is but one Lord, Jesus Christ, through whom all things came and through whom we live. But not everyone knows this. Some people are still so accustomed to idols that when they eat such food they think of it as having been sacrificed to an idol, and since their conscience is weak, it is defiled. (I Corinthians 8:4-7, NIV)

In this passage, Paul distinguishes between the object itself and the relationship taken to the object. After Paul denies that idols even exist, he writes, with the rhetorical flourish of conditionally assuming the very thing he just denied, "For even if there are so-called gods, whether in heaven or on earth (as indeed there are many 'gods' and many 'lords')." The many gods and many lords to which he refers are not objects, but relationships that we create—Hosea's "kings and princes" that are of our choosing not God's. So although there are no idols in the world, we can and do relate idolatrously. Nearly anything and everything can be the target of our idolatry.

If we reduce idolatry to a remote problem for ancient Israelites worshiping Ashtaroth or Baal, and ignore the sweeping prevalence of idolatry in society, the church, and our lives, we do so at our peril. However, to do so serves a useful purpose: it keeps us from seeing the frequency with which we create idolatrous relationships with people and things around us. It blinds us to the truth that all idolatry is self-worship: to desire to be the master rather than the servant.

Why worship the creation rather than the Creator? Why did the ancient Israelites ever turn from the Living God to worship the Ashtaroth (the symbols for the stars which the Canaanites worshiped) or Baal (the Phoenician god of the sun)? Why worship the stars or the sun? Certainly not because of ignorance of astronomy, but because by worshiping the creation rather than the Creator, we can be masters rather than servants.

Consider the idolatry of the Israelites camping at the foot of Mount Sinai. They stopped there three months after escaping from Egypt through the Red Sea. In the nineteenth chapter of Exodus, Moses received a reminder from the Lord for the people:

> Thus you shall say to the house of Jacob and tell the sons of Israel: "You yourselves have seen what I did to the Egyptians, and how I bore you on eagles' wings, and brought you to Myself. Now then, if you will indeed obey My voice and keep My covenant, then you shall be My own possession among all the peoples, for all the earth is Mine; and you shall be to Me a kingdom of priests and a holy nation." These are the words that you shall speak to the sons of Israel. (Exodus 19:3-6).

The people responded with an unanimous "Amen"—"All that the Lord has spoken we will do!" No problem!

However, after Moses disappeared on Mount Sinai for 40 days to receive the Ten Commandments and the design for the Tabernacle, the people grew weary of waiting for Moses to return. They approached Aaron and asked him to make them an idol to worship.

The speed and boldness of this request seems as surprising as Aaron's quick agreement. How could they so quickly turn from such dramatic displays of God's power in delivering the Israelites from the hand of Pharaoh? To learn anything from this incident, we must lay aside any judgment of how different we are from the Israelites and must embrace our similarities.

What can we learn from this episode at Mount Sinai? First, the people's request of Aaron, the first high priest, was "to make us a god. . .for *this Moses, the man who brought us up from the land of Egypt,* we do not know what has become of him" (Exodus 32:1, italics added). Their idolatry began when they thought that Moses rather than God had brought them from Egypt! This illustrates the idolatry to which they'd already fallen prey—what Schlossberg called "substitution of what is created for the creator." They were willing to worship anyone or anything other than this terrifying, mysterious God who had brought them out of Egypt and called them to responsible living!

Symbiotic Leadership

By creating an idolatrous relationship, we either make another person responsible for our lives or we choose to take responsibility for the lives of others. This symbiotic relationship defines the leadership model in our churches and society.

In many churches, pastors accept responsibility for the lives of their parishioners and the parishioners gladly make the pastor responsible for their lives. A sure indication of this hierarchical leadership model is the sense of ownership that the pastor has for "his flock." The pastor believes he must keep his congregation safe from outside influences which might lead them astray.

This attitude breeds an exclusivity—the pastor isolates his congregation from "dangerous" influences. The congregation in turn pledges "loyalty" to the pastor and the denomination. As a result of this lack of cross-pollination, the church style becomes rigid and calcified. This form, too, can become an idol. Look at what happens whenever a different style of worship or a different small group structure is introduced! In just our own limited experience we have seen this happen when church members take the *Momentus* training we offer.

Over the past five years, we have had numerous conversations with pastors who forbid the people in their church from attending a *Momentus* training. Often we find that the pastor's concern is not based on any direct experience with our ministry, but is more preventative—*just in case Momentus* is "not from God." This caution demonstrates the pastors' basic mistrust of their congregation's ability to govern themselves and keep themselves from harm's way.

In believing that it is their job, by virtue of their position and authority, to think for their congregations, pastors begin to view the liberty of people in the church as a threat. Liberty is mistaken as license, perhaps because the basic tools that equip one for self-government—accountability and true responsibility—are not active in their congregations.

Blind submission to anyone, even one's pastor, reveals an idolatrous relationship. When the congregation's idealization of the pastor is matched by the pastor's suspicion of anything "not invented here," there are real problems. If any outside influence or ministry is permitted, it must pass a tough doctrinal litmus test, which if not met results in the rejection of the whole ministry. With this paranoid attitude, pastors cut off possible contributions from other ministries.

The Bereans stand in stark contrast to most church goers today. When they received Paul and Silas—luminaries of the faith by anyone's measure—they "received the word with great eagerness" and examined "the Scriptures daily, to see whether these things were so" (Acts 17:11). The Bereans did not surrender their own responsibility to test what Paul and Silas were teaching, even though as apostles, Paul and Silas should have known what they were talking about. As a result, the Bereans were called "noble-minded."

How often today do we search the scripture to test what the pastor says? How often do we think for ourselves? Or do we leave the "testing of the spirit" to someone else, such as a third-party "research" organization?

Another consequence of the way pastors and church members relate is that unrealistic expectations are placed on pastors by their parishioners. Congregations put pastors on pedestals; some so high that the only way down is a devastating fall. Their unrealistic expectations result in a Virginia reel of people switching churches, finding their "ideal church home," becoming disillusioned, and switching once again.

The modern welfare state has developed a similar symbiotic relationship between those in authority and "the rank-and-file." The Government takes responsibility for the lives of citizens, and citizens eagerly surrender. Thus we have programs like Social Security that presume to take the responsibility for preparing for retirement. The rank-and-file leave the job of testing the suitability of policies and actions to third-party experts. They view the government as a vehicle to solve all of society's social problems, leaving the individual's sole contribution to its maintenance to be his tax dollars.

The myth that drives both of these theories is that someone can think for us; that someone is better at governing each of our lives than we are. This confusion of responsibility leads to many meaningless disputes. Being part of the "para-church," we at Mashiyach Ministries run into this with many pastors. One even went so far as to demand that a parishioner renounce his involvement with the *Momentus* training or leave the church. No amount of asking him to meet with me (Dan) to discuss his concerns bore fruit.

The pastor's idea of submission was defined as unconditional obedience. If the *Momentus* training was as dangerous as he apparently believed, then he had an obligation to research the accusations and rumors on which he was founding his decisions. The fact that he did not was a breach of his implied promise to love his neighbor as himself. Not only did he not love me, but he did not love his parishioner either.

Submission to authority (as described in Romans 13) or to husbands by their wives (mentioned in Ephesians 5) cannot be what this pastor believes it to be. The word "submission" in Greek means "a sense of being persuaded (whether rightly or wrongly) to a point of view." Nothing in the definition implies the condoning of pastoral "rank-pulling." This kind of power play, based solely on position, reveals an idolatrous relationship with form and structure.

We will explore the topic of submission to authorities at greater length in another book. For our purposes here, we will limit ourselves to a brief discussion of the prices and payoffs reaped by submission to this type of hierarchical relationship. This kind of relationship between pastors and congregations can only be kept in place by mutual agreement. It is also at the root of much of the tension and strife which seethes under the surface of many church communities—the tension that often leads to church schisms.

The congregation barters its principles for acceptance, and as part of the package buys someone to blame whenever it is unhappy. The pastor's payoff is a sense of certainty and the illusion of control. The pastor can feel that he is doing his job protecting "his flock" because his church is in order. The downside for the pastor is rapid burnout; a continual resentment as his congregation becomes more and more passive with few active leaders. For congregants, the price is disappointment in leaders and, if a congregant aspires to be a leader, an unfulfilled need to be recognized and invited into the leadership ranks. Everyone pays a price. As a result of this idolatry, the impact of the church on society is diminished.

On the Knife-Edge

Idolatry, for the ancient Israelites and for us today, comes from an unwillingness to depend on God in each moment. Idolatry is therefore a manifestation of unbelief. Living on the knife-edge of dependence on God is uncomfortable. In order to free themselves of their discomfort, the Israelites wanted something concrete and substantial to uphold their faith. We, too, rather than being satisfied by God's provision in the moment, desire structure to bring continuity to our relationship with Him. At first this structure helps us relate, but then it slowly consumes the relationship. We begin to depend on the structure to keep the relationship alive.

Whenever we create a relationship such that our internal condition depends on the external circumstances we are indulging in idolatry. Say for instance that you really want a new Mazda Miata. Not only do you want it, you can't live without it. Every time you see a Miata on the road, you can't help but notice how nice it looks. You just *know* how cool you'd look tooling around town with the top down. You must have it! Without that car you will be incomplete; only by having it can you be happy. You may think this is an exaggeration. But every day we convince ourselves that we need something or someone outside of ourselves to make us happy.

This movement from outside to inside, having what is outside of us determine who we are on the inside, is ultimately the movement of the victim. Victims always believe that they are helpless. Webster defines the word 'victim' as "one that is acted upon and usually adversely affected by a force or agent or one that is injured, destroyed, or sacrificed under any of various conditions." This is the way the word is used today. Historically however, the word 'victim' means "a living being sacrificed to a deity or in the performance of a religious rite."

Both meanings share the common thread of confusing the internal with the external. Being a victim in the modern sense of being oppressed, injured and so on, is a way of relating that views subjective experience (thoughts, feelings, and ways of relating with others) as dependent on something external. Unfortunately, when our internal condition depends on external circumstances, we will be victimized by whatever is going on around us.

A victim can also be a living being sacrificed to a deity. Sacrifices are offered to make someone or something holy. For example, the Levitical sacrifices were made to make the people of Israel holy. A victim makes holy the person or thing to which it is sacrificed. Another way to say this is that the victim makes his idol worthy and significant and important by the sacrifice of himself. This definition of a victim reveals the power and pervasiveness of idolatry in our society.

A Society of Victims

The victim uses fear to sensationalize adverse circumstances in order to extort and threaten others. This extortion lies behind much of the litigation pursued in the courts today: we are often encouraged to file a suit and shake some money out of someone or some company.

The modern materialistic spirit also relies on a similar hysteria to manipulate those who love to be victims into buying into victimhood. The culture sells the victim on the belief that a power outside of her can so overcome a her mind and being that the only recourse is to learn about it and stay away from it. This is the accusation that people are being "brainwashed," manipulated by "mind control," and swept into cults.

Whole organizations have been built on the idea that "brainwashing" and "mind control" are not only possible, but pose a real threat to people's liberty. These groups have bought the same snake oil that the culture sells the other victims. Despite the lack of evidence or a scriptural basis that brainwashing is even possible, these organizations warn others of the dangers of falling into the hands of the brainwashers. *They* would prefer to be the ones controlling the actions and thoughts of others.

The existence of a cult, as these groups define the term, rests on the assumption that somebody can manipulate circumstances, the environment, or information in such a way that the victim has no control over what he thinks or does, except to follow the leader's every wish. The testimony of both history and scripture belie the assertion that anyone can be hypnotized, manipulated through the environment, threatened, or tortured to surrender their will. The question really is how much you are willing to risk for your faith. The witnesses of such martyrs as Stephen, Joan of Arc, and the thousands of Christians who died in the Roman Colosseum, clearly show that those that are willing to die for their faith are not controlled by others. Modern examples of saints living in liberty include Richard Wurmbrand's 13 years of being tortured for Christ in a Communist prison and Corrie Ten Boom's experiences first as protector of the Jews and then as a captive in Nazi concentration camps. From the point of view of the victim, these examples teach nothing of faith or the power of Christ within us.

Several scriptures, including II Corinthians 11:10 ("As the truth of Christ is in me, no man shall stop me of this boasting in the regions of Achaia"), John 10:29 ("My Father, which gave them me, is greater than all; and no man is able to pluck them out of my Father's hand"), and I John 4:4 ("Ye are of God, little children, and have overcome them: because greater is he that is in you, than he that is in the world") indicate that no one, other than the Christian himself, can overcome the liberty Christ plants in the heart. The victim, whether she be Christian or not, is saying that she can be overcome by some external force; she fears being offered up as a sacrifice to some strange god! A victim buying into the superstitions of brainwashing and mind control are once again accusing God the way Adam and Eve did, by pointing the finger to external circumstances and assuming that God is not in them and has withheld Himself from them.

Imagining that there is a power outside of us greater than the power of God's Spirit in us allows us to do whatever is necessary to protect ourselves from the terrifying experience of being overcome by somebody's evil. Almost any selfish action can be rationalized as just and acceptable in the face of such a threat.

Every 'cult' phenomenon—from Jim Jones to Waco to the Inquisitions—reveals this similarity: the people involved wanted someone to take care of them the way they did not believe God would. The participants in such tragedies were unwilling to accept the liberty Christ won for them to govern their lives. These people made idols of men and ideas, and bought with their lives the illusion that somebody else would govern their lives better than they. Like the Israelites, they preferred the predicable comfort of Egyptian slavery, instead of living on the knife's edge in the promised land with God as their provider!

Serving an Appearance

'Idolatry' is a fascinating word that came straight into the English language from the Classical Greek word *eidololatreia*. It is composed of the two root words *eidos* (a variant of which is the source of our word "idol") and *latreia*, a word that will be examined presently. Let's first examine the word *eidos*. *Eidos* is defined as:

> The act of seeing, the thing seen, external appearance, sight; the object of sight, form, appearance; manner, kind, species....it refers to the visible appearance of things which are set in contrast to that which directs faith, meaning that the believer is guided not only by what he beholds, but by what he knows to be true though invisible.[29]

This phenomenal definition lays out the contrast between the victim and the victor. The victim looks to appearances or forms. How often is our life guided by the thing seen—the external appearance, the manner, kind, or species—instead of by the true but invisible? How often is our love based on what we see rather than by what we don't see? The church is by no means free from this sin! Many in the church today look solely at the appearance of things. Is the form correct? Do the outward signs line up with our own expectations? How often

---

[29] Spiros Zodhiates, *The Complete Word Study Dictionary: New Testament*, 507.

do we agree or disagree based on the surface, the outward form, with no regard to the unseen heart?

Whenever superstition and suspicion rear their ugly heads, we see the idol of form being worshiped. "Well, this doesn't look like what we do in our fellowship, therefore, it must be wrong. Better avoid that group, they don't teach what we do." Webster's 1828 Dictionary defines suspicion as follows:

> The imagination of the existence of something without proof, or upon very slight evidence, or upon no evidence at all. Suspicion often proceeds from the apprehension of evil: it is the offspring or companion of jealousy.[30]

Webster goes on and quotes a man named South to clarify the power of this spirit of suspicion:

> Nature itself, after it has been done an injury, will ever be suspicious, and no man can love the man he suspects.[31]

Another result of the idolatry of form is superstition. The definition of superstition in Webster's 1828 Dictionary is revealing because it gives insight into the foundation of suspicion. It reads:

> Excessive exactness or rigor in religious opinions or practice: extreme or unnecessary scruples in the observance of religious rites not commanded, or of points of minor importance, excess or extravagance in religion; the doing of things not required by God, or abstaining from things not

---

[30]Noah Webster, *Dictionary of the American Language.*

[31]Ibid.

forbidden; or the belief of what is absurd, or belief without evidence. [32]

What we value most determines our identity. If I value my own safety then I'll view every relationship a threat. I will ultimately suspect everybody I get into relationship with because I can not control the way they behave, the things they do or how they do them.

The complaint leveled against Mashiyach Ministries by watchdog organizations boils down to this argument: we are pursuing noble aims (love and transformation of character) but in a form that is tainted because it is similar to forms and exercises used by secular "new age" groups. This argument is concerned with the appropriate appearances; the concern is not with the fruit produced ("A good tree cannot produce bad fruit, nor can a bad tree produce good fruit," Matthew 7:18) or the intent and attitude of the heart. ("Not what enters into the mouth defiles the man, but what proceeds out of the mouth, this defiles the man," Matthew 15:11).

Rather than warning people away from 'dangerous' groups—an action based on fear and leads to schisms, these organizations that now exist solely to serve in a watchdog capacity could instead support the unity of the body of Christ. In love, they could assist people in pursuing reconciliation. Whether we like it or not, whether we agree or not on doctrinal issues, as long as we hold to the basic tenets of the Christian faith, we *will* be together for eternity! Why not seek understanding *now*?

---

[32]Ibid.

Service for Hire

Idolatry involves the appearance of things. But this is only half of the root word for idolatry. The second root is the word *latreia*, which means 'to worship; service for hire or as a slave.' It is distinct from *doulos*, which means bond-slave (a slave whose will was altogether consumed by the will of his master).

Idolatry is the relationship of worshiping an appearance *for hire*. There is an exchange involved. The worship is a transaction; in idolatry, we receive back something from our worship of the idol or appearance. What is the pay-off? Think about it. We make a distinction between a mercenary soldier and a voluntarily enlisted soldier. The mercenary fights for money. His allegiance goes to the highest bidder; he fights for the best deal. His allegiance to the uniform he wears is only skin-deep. It is not heart-felt. It does not spring from a sense of honor or duty. Character is not involved. The soldier takes his meaning from the form; he is not fighting out of principle. The volunteer, on the other hand, is fighting against the enemy because of a heartfelt commitment, because of principle, because of honor and conscience.

Since the Second World War, America has not fought a war from such principles. The idea is becoming foreign to us. We are so trapped by appearances, that we have no sense of anything deeper. We, like Narcissus, are enamored of our own reflection in the pond. As a culture and as Christians, we have fallen into a profound narcissism that searches everywhere for a reflection, an appearance, that will validate what we hope our image is, rather than creating a vision and sending it forth as promises.

Very often, narcissism prevents the examination of deeper issues. The form becomes so engrossing that all else is lost. In fact, the form and appearance is all we see; nothing else gets through. Idolatry is a *way of relating* to a person or thing, such that the idol defines who we are.

If we worship what is created rather than the creator, we corrupt the purpose for which we are created. If, as the Shorter Westminster Catechism says, "The highest end of man is to worship God and enjoy Him forever,"[33] then worshiping a creature leads inevitably to despair and victimhood. However, when we worship the Creator who made us, we throw off the chains of victimhood and live according to God's design. We acknowledge and allow the unique skills and capabilities He created in us to blossom.

Interrupting Idolatry

Idolatry and despair are bedfellows, because whenever we relate idolatrously to a form, appearance or person, we place our hope outside of ourselves. As the Psalm says, "Hope deferred makes the heart sick" (Proverbs 13:12). Our visions become a reality, only when we place our hope in our own ability to give of ourselves—not in someone or something external. Whenever we wait for a miracle to make our vision reality instead of pursuing our vision in action, despair envelopes us.

Two conditions interrupt despair. The first is having our identity formed from within; in other words, knowing who we are independent of other people or circumstances. This condition requires us to embrace all of who we are, including those aspects we dislike about ourselves. Having our identity formed from within, not without, defines the life of the victor and kills the victim inside. If the declaration of our vision,

---

[33]Answer to Question 1 in the Shorter Westminster Catechism.

dreams, and whole life and the sending of ourselves to another in promise kills idolatry, then the opposite action must define idolatry. The opposite action would include not declaring my vision, not sharing my dreams, guarding my life from pain and discomfort by playing it safe, not making promises, not risking rejection by withholding requests, and dishonestly hiding my bitterness behind the appearance of contentment.

The victim's identity depends on others and makes him wish he were different. In effect, the victim says, "I dislike who I am; my identity is bad, shameful, or defective. Therefore, I will be whoever someone else or some other circumstance tells me I am." In idolatry we refuse to be who God created us to be. We force ourselves to be someone else: more beautiful, less moody, more intelligent, better with people, more outgoing. Think of all the hooks and slogans used in advertising: youth, beauty, acceptance, sex appeal, 'Be all that you can be,' 'Have it your way,' 'You deserve a break today'—each of these appeals to the victim in us. They represent footholds for all sorts of idolatrous relationships.

Crisis of Hope

The victim lives in a crisis of hope. The victim believes circumstances prevent the vision he has of his life from being realized and fears that the circumstances will never change. If his hope that life can be different still flickers, he believes that someone or something else is the agent for the circumstances changing.

Without hope that he can change the circumstances such as by "stepping out" and letting God meet him, his vision becomes a fantasy—something nice when and if it happens, but nothing to stake your future on. For the victim, the circumstances determine his vision. When through a fortuitous alignment of circumstances the victim realizes his vision, he is not satisfied because he knows he cannot reproduce it. Nothing the victim did caused the vision to happen; therefore he superstitiously credits his vision to blind luck.

The focus on value in our culture, which is revealed by our society's concern over increasing self-esteem and self-worth, masks the deeper issue of hope. Where and in what do we place our hope? Is it within our God-given power to change reality through promise? Or do we place our hope in someone or something else changing so that our vision plops in our laps?

Our value falls into place when we handle the issue of hope. By bolstering value without having hope, we risk the temptation of believing that we must handle our own problems before we can love our neighbor. Figuring out how to love ourselves adequately before we love others is a red-herring. We delay ourselves in a trackless morass of relativity, asking ourselves the question, Have I loved myself enough yet?

I (Derek) know of a woman, let's call her Stacy, who has a grown daughter and a teenage son. This woman defines herself by her son, Stephen. Everything Stacey thinks and does ties back to her relationship with Stephen. She even refers to herself as 'Stephen's mother.' This leads to frequent disappointment. Because Stephen is now in high school and trying to break away from her, the smooth relationship they'd had is now fraught with conflict and brings her feelings of despair and hopelessness.

In allowing Stephen to define who she is, Stacy has placed herself in a "no win" situation. Reorienting her life without him as the center is terrifying. She fears that the alternative to having Stephen as her idol is to lose all relationship with him.

To see the dynamic in our own lives we must realize that the way we relate to everyone and everything around us fluctuates every moment. Like the saying, "you never step into the same stream twice," our relationships are always changing. From moment to moment, our way of relating to an object or person may move from idolatrous to responsible and back again. Not only is idolatry determined moment to moment, the variety of idolatry may change.

The Lust of the Eyes, Lust of the Flesh, and the Boastful Pride of Life

John divides "the world" into three parts, each of which is a form of idolatry. He writes,

> Do not love the world, nor the things in the world. If anyone loves the world, the love of the Father is not in him. For all that is in the world, the lust of the flesh and the lust of the eyes and the boastful pride of life, is not from the Father, but is from the world. And the world is passing away, and also its lusts; but the one who does the will of God abides forever. 1 John 2:15-18

The world (*kosmos*, in Greek) stands in opposition to God. Without repentance, the heart will assume one of the three attitudes enumerated by John. Putting this verse in today's vernacular, we would equate these to feeling good, looking good, and being right. Each of these attitudes of heart attempts to provide a sense of security—the sense of being in control and therefore being God. Each of them gets in the way of loving others as Christ loves us.

These three are comprehensive categories. All sin and all idolatry falls under one of these three. Each of these is an instance of greed—coveting what we don't have but think we desperately need.

The lust of the flesh is more than sexual; it is the desire to feel good, to be comfortable, to be unperturbed by the ravages of emotions, and to have all the desires of our flesh satisfied. The lust of the flesh is more than the ravenous urge in each of us for satisfaction. It is coupled with an attitude that will not be content unless the gaping maw is filled. The lust of the flesh manifests itself in a desire for money and power, which are surrogates for all that the flesh lusts after. With money and power, the other urges can be filled; not only filled, but filled in a way that also satisfies the urge to look good, which is the second category of idolatry.

Remember the popular bumper sticker that reads, "You can never be too rich or too thin"? Women still use the phrase with a laugh while their daughters throw up behind closed doors on college campuses because they're ashamed of their bodies or get arrested for shoplifting to look richer than they are! Being of an average thinness and average wealth is not good enough. Greed covets what we don't have but what we *think* we need. Paul also connects greed and idolatry. He urged the Colossians to "Therefore consider the members of your earthly body as dead to immorality, impurity, passion, evil desire, and greed, which amounts to idolatry" (Colossians 3:5).

The payoff of idolatry is the desire to have more of what the idol represents. Think of the calf that the Israelites created while Moses was on Mount Sinai. What was the payoff? What could a golden calf possibly bring them if not the payoff of the comfort and convenience that comes from creating our own god? The comfort of subjectivity; of never having our life interrupted by the objectivity of the physical universe? God had demonstrated his absolute and terrifying power to the Israelites when He delivered them from Egypt. He interrupted their subjectivity with the cloud of smoke and the pillar of fire. But when Moses tarried on the mountain, the Israelites substituted a molten calf for the real living God and declared that the calf was "your god, O Israel, who brought you up from the land of Egypt." The Israelites exchanged the dangerous, unpredictable, spontaneous, living God for an appearance, a form that would never interrupt the slavery of a subjective interpretation of God that was comfortable and known.

Our idols may not be as obvious to us as the molten calf. We may worship the idol of doctrinal correctness and conformity—a dogmatic insistence on certain nonessential tenets of the Christian faith—and thereby fall under the third category of idolatry. This category is "being right" or the pride of life about which John wrote. We not only have an overwhelming desire to be right, but we want people to *know* that we are right. How many denominations do we have in this country alone? How many churches have split over doctrinal struggles? These struggles get their divisive energy from the idol of being right.

Often in doctrinal quarrels the outward form, which is what is plainly visible in life, is identified as the source of the quarrels and differences that divide the body. James asked the question:

> What is the source of quarrels and conflicts among you? Is not the source your pleasures that wage war in your members? You lust and do not have; so you commit murder. And you are envious and cannot obtain; so you fight and quarrel. You do not have because you do not ask. You ask and do not receive, because you ask with wrong motives, so that you may spend it on your pleasures. You adulteresses, do you not know that friendship with the world is hostility toward God? Therefore whoever wishes to be a friend of the world makes himself an enemy of God. (James 4:1-4)

What is the source of the quarrels, the differences that separate believer from believer, person from person? James lays it to lust and the compulsion to satisfy pleasures. These are payoffs for idolatry. When we desire to love others as God has loved us, by making promises and keeping them, then our quarreling will cease. Making and keeping promises interrupts the subjective rationalizations and greedy desires of the soul by drawing our attention away from ourselves toward God and others.

Whenever the form becomes significant to us, we are being idolatrous. Whenever we put on an appearance for someone, we are worshiping an idol! Whenever we are concerned about an image that is not fully revealing of our authentic soul, we are serving an idol. When we believe that the form matters or is significant, we are serving an idol. This is what the Scripture means when it talks about taking on a form of godliness but denying the power thereof.

7. Transformation of Heart and Character

But now abide faith, hope, love, these three; but the greatest of these is love.

I Corinthians 13:13

The temptation to relate to others as a victim plagues each of us. Indeed, it often seems inevitable. But must we endure this for all our days or is there hope for transformation?

The hope for a radical transformation of heart and character lives in each of us. But although radical transformation is possible, what is not possible is a permanent change—being so different that we cannot be the same again *ever* (at least in this life). That type of transformation is found only in the movies.

The movie series *Back to the Future* played with this idea. The young hero of the movie, Marty McFly, goes back in time and inadvertently interrupts his parents' courtship, thereby threatening his life (because if his parents don't marry, he won't be born). Overcoming many mishaps, he reignites his parents' love and returns to the future to find that his nerdy, brow-beaten father has become a very successful science fiction writer because of Marty's interference.

All of us desire this type of permanent change for ourselves and others, but it is not possible in this life—God does not provide it nor can we accomplish it. To believe that we could accomplish it would be to believe that man is able to perfect himself in this world. We could move from one "permanent" change to the next until we need change no more. If we read the Scriptures with this hope, we can even find some support for it: for example, II Corinthians 5:17 "Therefore if any man is in Christ, he is a new creature; the old things passed away; behold, new things have come" and I Samuel 10:6, wherein Samuel prophesies over Saul that "the Spirit of the Lord will come upon you mightily, and you shall prophesy with them and be changed into another man." However, even a cursory review of Saul's life reveals that in no way was his transformation permanent. His transformation required, as ours does, his ongoing commitment to maintain it.[34]

The ongoing commitment required in transformation is indicated by the verb tense Paul used. In the second letter to the Corinthians, the verb tense in Greek is *present continuous*, which might be better rendered, "all things become and are becoming new." The transformation of character is ongoing, whereas salvation is an event.

There are two possibilities for transformation, each represented by a different Greek word in the New Testament. The first type of change is *metaschematizo*, which means changing the form, the schematic, the scenery, the appearance; the second is *metamorphoo*, changing the heart or essence. Vine's Expository Dictionary describes *metamorphoo*, which is the word for 'transformed' in Romans

---

[34]Transformation is different from anointing; just as for us transformation is distinct from salvation. Until Saul's death, David would not raise a hand against him because Saul still was anointed by God. Likewise, salvation is different from transformation — salvation dealing with our eternal state and transformation (once called "sanctification") with how we relate in the here and now.

12:2 ("be transformed by the renewing of your mind . . ."), as follows:

> the obligation being to undergo a complete change which, under the power of God, will find expression in character and conduct; *morphe* lays stress on the inward change.[35]

We use the transliterated word *metamorphosis* in English to denote an internal change of heart.

Metaschematizo and *metamorphoo* can be contrasted as follows:

> The outward [change of appearance] is best illustrated by contrasting *metaschematizo* with *metamorphoo* . . . . If one were to change a Japanese garden into an Italian one, this would be *metaschematizo*. But if one were to transform a garden into something wholly different, as a ball-field, it is *metamorphoo*. It is possible for Satan to *metaschematizo*, transform himself into an angel of light, i.e., he can change his whole outward semblance. But it would be impossible to apply *metamorphoo* to any such change for this would imply an internal change, a change not of appearance but of essence, which lies beyond his power.[36]

Metaschematizo always deals in the paradigm of incremental change—moving from moment to moment in the hope that in the next moment we will have slightly more of what we

---

[35]W.E. Vine, et al., *Vine's Complete Expository Dictionary of Old and New Testament Words*, 639.

[36]Spiros Zodhiates, *The Complete Word Study Dictionary: New Testament*, 973.

want, to be better in a certain way, and to be incrementally different. More, better, and different. These markers will show up in your language whenever you live in this paradigm. For example, "Son, you need to work more diligently at your studies." Or, "I want to have a better relationship with you." Or, "I think our team needs to develop a different set of skills."

The implication or presupposition in each of these is that the way we are giving ourselves to the situation is basically sound: Our relationship is good, but we just need to make it a little better; our sons and daughters already are applying themselves with diligence, a little more of the same will produce the outcomes we envision; the team has all the skills it needs—they just need to use them more effectively. The world of *metaschematizo* never shows up as a radical break with our history. It implies a two-dimensional world with no conception of a third dimension. Like someone facing the famous Nine Dot Problem[37] for the first time, we never break from our own self-imposed shackles.

With a *metamorphosis*, we gain altitude and see our situation from different perspectives; we are able to expand our horizons beyond, over, and under our previous limitations. We find out what it means to have a problem rather than the problem having us.

These two types of transformation correspond to relating as victims or victors. *Metaschematizo* perpetuates the victim's way of relating. Nothing changes but the content—*what* the person is a victim *to*. The victim may want a true change of heart, a *metamorphosis*, as we all do, but he pursues it

---

[37] Connect all the dots with four straight lines, do not retrace lines or lift your pen:

    ● ● ●

    ● ● ●

    ● ● ●

through the fruitless approach of changing forms and appearances. He does not see that *metamorphosis* must come first; it is the doorway out of the bondage of being a victim.

Once the victor enters a responsible relationship with others, *metaschematizo* comes to bear. *Metaschematizo* is critical to the process of reaching another with our commitment—being willing to shift the packaging in order for our vision for the other person to be realized. Paul describes the *metaschematizo* he pursued after his *metamorphosis* on the road to Damascus in this way:

> For though I am free from all men, I have made myself a slave to all, that I might win the more. And to the Jews I became as a Jew, that I might win Jews; to those who are under the Law, as under the Law, though not being myself under the Law, that I might win those who are under the Law; to those who are without law, as without law, though not being without the law of God but under the law of Christ, that I might win those who are without law. To the weak I became weak, that I might win the weak; I have become all things to all men, that I may by all means save some. (I Corinthians 9:19-22)

The key difference between the victim's use of *metaschematizo* and Paul's is the heart from which he changed and, thus, who the transformation benefited. The victim's *metaschematizo* serves himself (which is always what someone endeavoring to be the master of his world wants). The victim changes his appearance in order to look good, to be accepted and right, to feel good, or to be in control—his heart is imbedded deep in idolatry. Paul's heart, on the other hand, was to serve; his *metaschematizo* was for the benefit of others.

The three building blocks of *metamorphosis* from victim to victor is founded on three building blocks: hope in a vision, faith that God will provide, and love for others. We will examine each of these building blocks separately, although they coexist and inextricably mingle with each other. In the next chapter, we will discuss practical tools for transforming from victim to victor and maintaining the *metamorphosis*.

Faith that God Will Provide

The *metamorphosis* from victim to victor begins with hope. The victim strives to control himself, circumstances, and others in order to be a master; the victor is content to serve. The first span of the bridge over this huge gulf from victim to victor is vision. In order to hope, we must have a vision in which to place our hope.

For a word that is used so widely in our society, "vision" is hard to pin down. It is a member of the class of nouns known as *nominalizations* or nouns that are derived from verbs. The problem with the tendency to nominalize in the English language is that we forget the original action that was frozen into the noun. Notice the difference in understanding made by turning a nominalization back into a verb. For example, you might say that "I am in love" or "I fell in love." With verbs instead of nouns, these sentences would become simply "I love" or "I am loving." Two things happen when the verb form of love is used: 1) it is clear that love is an action—a dynamic process, rather than a static state; and 2) the sense of motion in the verb calls for the object of love to be named.

Denominalizing "vision" from noun to verb is a little harder than the above example of love. Vision certainly has something to do with *visualizing* or *seeing*, specifically seeing what is not present at the moment, but what is possible in the future.

It is in the future orientation of vision that we can begin to see the connection between vision and faith. Vision is a precursor to faith. Vision sees the possibilities for the future and faith settles on one possibility and is fully persuaded that the chosen possibility will be realized.

How does this functional definition of vision fare biblically? In the Bible, the classic text on vision is found in Proverbs 29:18. The verse reads: "Where there is no vision, the people perish." This frequently quoted version leaves a mistaken impression: that vision is some kind of essential, but undefinable and subjective force. With this understanding, many people fool themselves into believing they have a vision by thinking, "without vision, whatever that is, I will perish; I haven't perished yet, so I must have vision!" This couldn't be further from the truth! Vision is not about mere survival; it has to do with our quality of life and our character, which in turn determines how we live. Vision makes the difference between playing to win and playing not to lose.

A more careful rendering of the Hebrew of this text reads "where there is no vision the people are unrestrained"; in other words they are *undisciplined*. If we do not pursue our vision with disciplined action, we will fall into despair. The hope of attaining the vision calls us to jettison every excess action and pare our lives down to the essentials that propel us along the path to our vision. Discipline towards a vision is not onerous! It is joyful, because it is filled with hope.

When, however, our vision does not overcome our own inertia, we despair. We begin to give up on our vision of a compelling future; we rationalize our lack of action, hoping that someone else will bring our vision to life. Very often this life of despair is more comfortable than the life of discipline required for the pursuit of a vision.

The life of comfort we exchange for our vision may not even seem that despairing. Rationalizations can be very comfortable. "After all," so the theory goes, "every dream can't come true." But in this despair we join Esau—we trade our inheritance (our vision) for a bowl of soup—for looking good, feeling good, or being right. We pursue our favorite flavor of self-gratification and we make one of these idols holy by the sacrifice of our vision. In fact, without a vision to bring constraint, we strive only for comfort. Comfort is the antithesis of vision, because vision calls us to delay gratification of our immediate desires in favor of the possibilities of the future. Unfortunately, despair is the state in which many people live.

The antithesis of comfort and vision is perhaps most easily seen in sports. I (Derek) swam competitively from the time I was nine through my college years. In high school and college, I trained rigorously—up to twenty-four hours a week through most of the year. In an average week we would swim between 60 to 70 kilometers in preparation for championship meets that occurred twice a year. At these meets, each of us would compete in perhaps ten events, most of which lasted less than two and a half minutes! It was the vision of winning those two championship meets that motivated the daily discipline of working out so strenuously. In a much more profound way, Jesus endured the rigors of the cross for the vision of the joy set before him (Hebrews 12:2).

Vision brings discipline, and discipline supplies a sense of purpose and meaning to life. The loss of vision and discipline is a fact of life for most Americans. They may not be perishing, but they are undisciplined, drifting, and aimlessly wandering. And while they are wandering, they wonder where the meaning to life has gone—assuming they can remember a time when their life had vital meaning!

The second hallmark of vision is that it leads to accomplishment, because of the *passion* of the visionary. Think about some of the recognizably visionary people in our cultural history: Martin Luther King, Jr., Gandhi, Helen Keller, Thomas Jefferson, Florence Nightingale, Abraham Lincoln, Marie Curie, Albert Einstein, Thomas Edison, Mother Theresa. What do these men and women have in common? It must be something besides discipline, or vision ends up sounding like a nun at a strict boarding school! One thing common to each of these people is that they accomplished something significant: new knowledge, a better way of doing things, or a technological, political, or social breakthrough.

Think of the visionary people at work, in your social circle, among your friends. Have you noticed that people who have a vision are passionate about it? True vision generates a lot of energy. Can you imagine one of these visionaries saying, "Ho hum, I guess it's just about time to get to one of the things that I really enjoy doing in life, but . . . that bed looks awfully inviting, maybe I'll crawl back in?" Not if they are men and women of great passion and energy.

Their passion connects their vision to their accomplishments. Passion moves vision out of the subjective and ephemeral, and into the physical and life-changing.

Gnosticism and Textualism

The wedding of passion and discipline creates a powerful tension for getting something significant done in our lives! Another way to describe this tension is *possibility* and *necessity*. All of us live in the tension between possibility and necessity, passion and discipline. We get ourselves in big trouble when we live for too long at either end of the spectrum. If we dwell strictly in the possibilities and are all passion—excited, revved up, lots of energy, but have no direction to channel that passion—we end up living a variation on the theme of "eat, drink, and be merry." We have our heads in the clouds but our feet are not on the ground. This wanton lifestyle is one variety of the despair that comes from seeing the future, but not pursuing a compelling vision. This is called "the despair of possibility." Action is overwhelmed by myriad possibilities. At the other end of this spectrum, if we see too few possibilities, we again take no action. This is "the despair of necessity."

Another common form of the despair of possibility is *gnosticism*. Gnosticism traditionally has referred to a belief system that focused on "private knowledge" (*gnosis* in Greek) for salvation. One consequence of gnosticism was a debasing of the physical as evil—only the spiritual is considered holy. In the church today, gnosticism continues. Modern gnosticism glorifies knowledge, generally subjective knowledge that comes directly from God. The current of gnosticism in the church runs deep. It surfaces in a variety of ways: in a focus on possibilities without ever moving into action, in an emphasis on subjective experience—nearly to the exclusion of correlating our experience with reality, in the urge to be right, and in "playing-not-to-lose."

The problem is *not* that waiting on God, or being right, or being prudent and cautious is gnostic. What is gnostic is if we require special revelation from God for direction before any action is taken. The source of vision for the future is always in the hearts of men and women. God has promised to be the source of prophetic visions (Joel 2:2), but we are talking about the more mundane vision that calls us out of bed each morning. Placing the responsibility on God for creating our vision provides both an excuse for inactivity and a ready out—since this is an exclusive personal revelation, no one else has the grounds to question or test it.

The scriptures are clear about what the hallmarks of the Christian's life ought to be. Jesus himself summed up all the scriptures in this way:

> 'You shall love the Lord your God with all your heart, and with all your soul, and with all your mind.' This is the great and foremost commandment. The second is like it, 'You shall love your neighbor as yourself.' On these two commandments depend the whole Law and the Prophets." (Matthew 22:37-40).

The direction and spirit—love God and love our neighbor—are clear. Furthermore, God has given each of us talents and brains to pursue these two commandments. He leaves it to us to pick a course to follow, then He guides us in the way we should go. The strategy is Matthew 10:16, "Behold, I send you out as sheep in the midst of wolves; therefore be shrewd as serpents, and innocent as doves."

One of the payoffs for the gnostic is the illusion of protection gnosticism provides. By being strictly reflective, the gnostic imagines that he is spared the difficult process of accounting for his actions—what he may have missed in hearing from God and what he may have added. Paul carried with him the pain of his persecution of the saints. By committing our whole heart to a particular direction, we open ourselves to whole-heartedly pursuing the "wrong" direction; that "wrong" direction often has consequences which do not evaporate once God sets us straight. But without embarking on the journey we can never say definitively which door would have been best to take, we can only remain speculative and reflective. The gnostic strategy gives us license to value our thoughts, emotions, and image above loving our neighbor in specific action.

A shining example of this gnostic trade-off was a call I (Larry) received from a friend. When I picked up the phone, I heard Gayle's voice. I had led a leadership workshop at her church. Gayle was involved in the prophetic ministry and called to tell me a dream she had about me. She tripped over her words as she told me the details of her dream—she had seen me in a homosexual affair. I assured her that homosexuality was not one of my struggles. Gayle did not accept my assurance, at first. She was convinced that her dream was true. Based on similar dreams in the past, this dream *seemed* of a similar nature. Convinced that this was a dream from God, Gayle was reluctant to change her opinion even in the face of my repeated assurances.

This is gnosticism at work. The gnostic prefers the internal and subjective over the external and objective. Christian gnosticism satisfies itself with all the glorious possibilities of life and all that God *could* do. However, only infrequently is Christian gnosticism moved to action. Rather, Christian gnostics remain in repose and reflection, considering all that *might* be done. At most, Christian gnosticism rises to outbursts of momentary excitement,[38] even fever-pitched excitement, before settling back into repose. The Christian gnostic satisfies himself with the consideration of action that rests in intentions, rather than results.

Textualism is an intellectual variant of gnosticism. The textualist is more interested in discoursing ideas than living them. So the textualist is satisfied in knowing *about* truths and is less concerned with experiencing the truth he knows. And since the focus is primarily knowledge, the community of believers suffers schisms over minor doctrinal differences.

---

[38]Søren Kierkegaard discusses this characteristic of modern life in *This Present Age*.

The emphasis in textualism shifts from the heart—whether we relate to people from our vision in love, or in fear—to the *form* that we use to talk about our hearts. Textualists judge the form of the words, rather than the heart behind them. This difference was abruptly brought home in some correspondence I (Dan) had with a writer and conference-speaker, whom I'll call Jeffrey.

I loved his books. I read and reread them. I especially appreciated his discussion on the nature of truth, the difference between knowing truth and being true to what one knows. He seemed to have a bead on textualism! He wrote powerfully about the difference between the two ways of living and the influence *being* true has on our relationship with God and others.

I finally had the occasion to meet him and we began to correspond. I was thrilled by what we were able to give to each other, until someone sent him a packet of information that was critical of our ministry. His next letter to me was guarded, distant and suspicious. He wrote that he was concerned that my previous letter contained language that was "new age," "self oriented," and "not the language of apostolicity." He went on to say:

> What I am sensing in the whole tone of [your] letter and particularly in some key phrases used, is an essential 'humanism' that is perceived as spirituality. The references to "inner longing," being "in touch with their longing," "the journey of life," "a pilgrimage toward wholeness," "an all embracing journey," "our deepest selves," etc., give me, frankly, a sense of disquiet. This is not the language of apostolicity nor indeed of Scripture, but rather the ego-centric pining of souls bent upon their own self-realization more than Christ's glory.

In his isolated focus on specific words, Jeffrey missed the attitude of my heart. The inner longing in our hearts—our journey—is not toward self-fulfillment, but is the response to what one writer has called "the God-shaped void in our hearts."

Imagine my sorrow; here was a man I respected and loved whose entire relationship with me was poisoned by misinformation sent out by a watch-dog organization. Instead of working with me to discover the truth, he became afraid of being deceived, which, in itself is a form of deception. The only answer to this fear is found in the grace and love of God. As we love one another, fear has no place, even the fear of being deceived.

In the book *Keys To The Deeper Life*, A.W. Tozer addresses the impact of textualism:

> Faith, a mighty, vitalizing doctrine in the mouths of the apostles, became in the mouth of the scribe another thing altogether and power went from it. As the letter triumphed, the Spirit withdrew and textualism ruled supreme. It was the time of the believer's Babylonian captivity.
>
> In the interest of accuracy it should be said that this was a general condition only. Certainly there were, even in those low times, those whose longing hearts were better theologians than their teachers were. These pressed on to a fullness and power unknown to the rest. But they were not many and the odds were too great; they could not dispel the mist that hung over the land. The error of textualism is not doctrinal. It is far more subtle than that and much more difficult to discover, but its effects are just as deadly. Not its theological beliefs are at fault but its assumptions.
>
> It assumes, for instance, that if we have the word for a thing we have the thing itself. If it is in the Bible, it is in us. If we have the doctrine, we have the experience. If something was true for Paul it is of necessity true of us

because we accept Paul's epistles as divinely inspired. The Bible tells us how to be saved, but textualism goes on to make it tell us that we are saved, something in the very nature of things it cannot do. Assurance of individual salvation is thus no more than a logical conclusion drawn from doctrinal premises, and the resultant experience wholly mental.[39]

The speed with which we isolate ourselves from others because of doctrinal differences is astounding. In many families, slight doctrinal differences become a wedge that separates brother from brother, sister from sister, and parents from children.

The schisms we create and perpetuate isolate us from the provision of God. How often do we turn from the women and men through whom God would bless us because they use different language, dress differently, or are not religiously correct to our way of thinking?

The scripture says:

Give, and it shall be given unto you; good measure, pressed down, and shaken together, and running over, shall men give into your bosom. For with the same measure that ye mete withal it shall be measured to you again. (Luke 6:38, KJV)

How can God use men and women to give into our bosoms if we are not willing to even listen to them? When textualism drives us from relating in love to our brothers and sisters, we enter despair.

Despair and death of the spirit live at both ends of the polemic. Because of a lack of a true vision of eternity with

---

[39]A.W. Tozer, *Keys to the Deeper Life*, 20-21.

Christ, both the gnostic and the textualist are like the man rearranging the deck chairs on the Titanic—they may look good, but they accomplish nothing of lasting significance. The ship still goes down.

Without discipline and passion in pursuing our vision for a meaningful future, we relegate ourselves to fulfilling the desires of the flesh, which lead to death. The early church fathers catalogued seven cardinal, or deadly sins: pride, rage, envy, greed, lust, gluttony, and sloth. These sins destroy love and vision; they are the tools of the victim.

The Source of Vision

So, how does vision come? The easy, but incomplete, answer is that vision comes spontaneously from God. This answer begs the question and is incomplete because vision and direction require a certain receptivity from us. Not the receptivity of gnosticism, but the receptivity that comes from being already in motion toward the vision.

When God directs His people, He does so in the journey, not while we reflect on the journey before we begin. This is the example of Saul on the road to Damascus. Many other priests persecuted the Christians. More still probably thought that the Christians *should be* persecuted and stoned as blasphemers. Why did Jesus appear to Saul and not another? Without the benefit of Jesus' word on this puzzle, we can only speculate that the other Pharisees were not pursuing God with their whole hearts the way Saul was. Even though he was moving 180 degrees against God, Jesus appeared to him and put him on the true path. Without Paul's abandon of heart to glorify God as best he could, the correction would not have come.

The Scriptures make clear that even under the old covenant, God's direction came in the journey. Proverbs 16 is one such passage:

> The plans of the heart belong to man, but the answer of the tongue is from the LORD. . . . Commit your works to the LORD, and your plans will be established. . . . The mind of man plans his way, but the LORD directs his steps. (Proverbs 16:1, 3, 9)

Each verse points to man's journey as the context for God's direction: the plans of the heart and committing the work to the Lord *are* the journey.

The structure of vision is distinct from the structure of talent. Vision implies a sole focus on realizing a future possibility in relationship with others. Vision requires a willingness to stand responsibly—and to transform the outward appearance to whatever extent is required to have the vision become a reality. The structure of talent starts out with a person's innate and unique skills and then moves from that base to finding out where those talents can best be put to use. Notice the different presuppositions in each: the structure of vision is dynamic, open-ended, generative; the structure of talent is close-ended, deterministic, limited—an expression of a fixed genetic endowment. What if a vision calls something forth for which the individual has no "talent"? People with a high level of accomplishment in their field will tell you that the bulk of their supposed "in-born talent" started out as generic human raw material. It was then honed to its highest level because of the vision they had, and the passion and discipline that came along with that vision.

The structure of vision calls out faith. This truth is revealed in Hebrews 11:1: "Now faith is the assurance of things hoped for, the conviction of things not seen." The Greek words translated "assurance" and "conviction" are fascinating. The word "assurance" is *hupostasis*, meaning:

> that which underlies the apparent, hence reality, essence, substance; that which is the basis of something, hence, assurance, guarantee, confidence.[40]

The first part of the verse can be restated, "faith is confidence in things hoped for." Being fully persuaded that things hoped for will be realized. Faith is the foundation of vision; it is what vision stands on between the time we declare it, and the time we accomplish it. Faith is required, because often there is nothing else to grasp. Whenever we declare a vision, we experience a dizzy feeling of hanging in the air without support. Faith is the support: a belief that with God all things are possible. Faith also is the test of a vision. The word for conviction in Hebrews 11:1 is *elengkos*:

> Conviction. Metonymically, meaning certain persuasion. In the sense of refutation of adversaries. Implies not merely the charge on the basis of which one is convicted, but the manifestation of the truth of that charge and the results to be reaped; also the acknowledgment, if not outwardly, yet inwardly, of its truth on the part of the accused. . . .By implication spoken of hidden things, detection, demonstration, manifest.[41]

---

[40] Spiros Zodhiates, *The Complete Word Study Dictionary: New Testament*, 1426.

[41] Ibid., 562.

Faith also serves as the proof of a vision. If you don't muster the faith, the vision will never happen; but if you believe wholeheartedly, passionately, with discipline, faith will bring that which is not seen into reality. Being fully persuaded refutes the charges of the adversary that unseen things are not real. Being fully persuaded involves surrendering to God's defense—that even though unseen things are not yet manifest, faith stands in the place of unseen things until they are manifest.

The nouns "faith" and "belief" are nominalizations—they are abstract nouns. We cannot point to them like we can point to a desk or a car. Nominalizations are always created from an action—they are action verbs that are frozen into nouns. The advantage of the word "belief" over the word "faith" is that in English, the noun "belief" corresponds to the verb "to believe"; the noun "faith" has no directly corresponding verb. With the word "faith," we will have to make do with the verb "to believe." We could say that faith *is* believing, just as freedom *is* being free and to be in love means loving.

The Greek word for faith is *pistis*. It is derived from the verb *peitho* which means "to win over, to persuade." *Pistis* is defined in this way:

> Faith. Subjectively meaning firm persuasion, conviction, belief in the truth, veracity, reality....Objectively meaning that which is believed, doctrine, the received articles of faith.[42]

The phrase "subjectively meaning firm persuasion, conviction, belief in the truth, veracity, reality" means our personal experience of faith; what faith is on the inside; that which

---

[42]Ibid., 1162.

comes before our ability to explain it in words, even to ourselves.

Because of Western culture's dedication to the principles of the scientific method, we revere the objective. Scientific method claims that a phenomenon is empirically real when an independent scientist observes the same phenomenon after performing the same series of steps. For example, during the hoopla several years ago about "cold fusion," other scientists had difficulty reproducing the initial results of the cold fusion researchers. Thus the scientific community concluded that there was no reality to the cold fusion claims. Reality is equated with the observable, the external, the mechanistic. So if something is observable, external, and mechanistic, it is considered to be objective. Things subjective of course then are just the opposite—not directly observable, but internal, ambiguous, open to interpretation. In a society oriented toward objectivity such as our own, the subjective is correspondingly degraded. How many times have you heard these derogatory comments . . . "he is not being objective," or "if you looked at this objectively, you would. . . .," or "Don't be so subjective."

In very important ways, this dominance of the objective is misleading. Being objective in the way the scientific method describes is an illusion. We are all inescapably and permanently trapped in our own subjective experience of external "objective" reality. No matter what we do, how careful, how scientific and calculating, no matter how detailed in our observing, we cannot avoid interpreting reality through our own subjective screen. Another metaphor for this process is to say that we do not experience the multidimensional, many-faceted, infinitely rich "objective" reality directly, but we construct a model of reality that we carry around with us.

Our subjective model of reality guides us. It is our "world-view." We only operate from our model of reality, never reality itself. At best, we can know when our subjective experience of reality is out of alignment with objective reality, when we are confronted with inconsistencies between the way we believe things are and the way they actually show up.

For example, when I (Derek) was young, I considered myself to be introverted. That was as significant feature of my map of reality. As a result, I didn't like parties. In college, I found that I enjoyed social activities more than I expected. This was disconcerting because my map did not agree with my experience.

Through feedback—our experience of reality around and in us—we can improve our map and fill in missing details. But no matter how attentive we are to all the feedback we can get our hands on, no matter how diligent and quick we are to make changes, we still do not approach an objective knowledge of reality.

The degree to which our subjectivity can lead us astray came home to me (Dan) in the winter of 1988. I was spending a lot of time away from home working both at ship brokering and designing the *Momentus* training. Aileen often told me how much she missed me and how she wished we could take the time to do something wonderful together. I answered her longing with assurances that this would soon be all over. She agreed that she'd be ok with that for awhile, but from time to time still mentioned her desire for more excitement.

Then in the beginning of December, she began to leave the house at unusual times. I would call home and find a sitter staying with the kids. When I asked her where she was going she said she was Christmas shopping. I did not see any presents anywhere, but shrugged it off.

Then one day she said she was meeting a friend for lunch. At noon that same friend called me looking for Aileen. "I thought she was having lunch with you," I said. There was silence on the other end of the phone. Then, a hurried, "Oh yeah, that's right I forgot, I better get on my way."

I was really suspicious now! I went home to look for presents. I found nothing except a card that read "Joe's" and a phone number written in her handwriting. When I called the number a man answered. I asked him what his name was and he said, "Joe why?" My hands started sweating. I hung up quickly. Could she be having some sort of affair with Joe?

I could not believe it! We'd been communicating so well! Perhaps she was so lonely that she was seeking companionship. I decided to take her to the movies. I arranged for somebody to sit with the children and called with my invitation. She turned me down because she was tired and had too much to do the next morning. I was devastated. Had someone else won her heart because I had neglected her?

I asked my business partner, Eric, if he had noticed anything unusual about Aileen. He said no. In fact he invited Aileen and me to have dinner with him and his wife the next night. I told him I didn't know if Aileen would be up for that as she had been quite busy, but I would ask. I decided I would confront Aileen about my fears the next night after dinner.

The next day Aileen said she had some errands to run before we went to dinner. Could she meet me at Eric's house? She said the sitter was coming earlier than we had planned. Visions of a pre-dinner *rendez-vous* with Joe grabbed me by the throat. I was curt with her on the phone, but I did not say anything. I obsessed all day about the evidence I had discovered. On the way to Eric's, I was quite subdued. He kept asking me if I was all right or if I needed something. I said no. Finally he stopped at a grocery store and took forever inside. I laid my head back and closed my eyes to try and relax. How was I going to ask the questions that were racing through my mind?

When Eric finally came back to the car, he said he wasn't feeling well. I thought, "Great! Aileen will probably be late coming from who knows where, Eric isn't feeling good, and I can't think of anything other than uncovering my wife's affair.

When we arrived at Eric's house in the country, it was quiet and peaceful. A soft light from the rising moon streamed across the lawn. The still evening soothed my nerves somewhat. I didn't notice much as we went through the front door and up the stairs. I dreaded seeing my wife. What would I say? Could my fears be true? My heart was so heavy I thought it would surely break when I saw her.

Imagine my astonishment when Eric turned on the lights and I heard a thunderous "SURPRISE!" One hundred of my closest friends—many whom I had not seen in years—stood there smiling and taking pictures. Aileen was standing over a magnificent cake at the table with tears in her eyes and a huge smile on her face.

I wept as I embraced my gracious, lovely wife. "You don't know how surprised I am," I managed to get out through my tears.

I admired the cake and asked her if she had made it. "No," she said, "I bought it at Joe's." All my subjective fears, which had seemed so real only moments before, dissolved in the reality of her shining love for me. All my suspicions had been baseless.

Only God himself knows objective reality; He *is* objective reality. We do have the hope and his promise that there will be a day that we will share an objective knowledge of reality. Our current subjectivity, and our eventual sharing of God's objective view of reality is what Paul speaks of in I Corinthians 13:

> For we know in part, and we prophesy in part; but
> when the perfect comes, the partial will be done

away. When I was a child, I used to speak as a child, think as a child, reason as a child; when I became a man, I did away with childish things. For now we see in a mirror dimly, but then face to face; now I know in part, but then I shall know fully just as I also have been fully known. (Corinthians 13:9-12)

Our permanent subjectivity impacts our faith. Faith is a subjective condition—that of *being fully persuaded.* This is a radically different definition of faith for most people. Faith as a noun tempts us to think of faith as a quantity. The question then becomes how much faith we have. Do we have enough? Or is it too little? How *much* is "faith as a grain of mustard seed"? If mustard seed is so small, the smallest of seeds; we don't need much to move mountains, do we? But don't we talk about men of great faith? Didn't Jesus have trouble healing in his home town because of their lack of faith? Describing faith using the metaphor of the grain of mustard seed clearly eliminates size as the defining criterion of faith.

Our concept of faith is taken captive by our use of language. Because the word "faith" is a noun, and a nominalization at that, we naturally think in terms of quantities. How different this is from thinking of faith as "being fully persuaded!" The question of faith is "Am I fully persuaded?" The answer is either yes or no.

Another consequence of the traditional view of faith is that we think of faith as something that we can store up. We think of faith as so many cans of soup that we can store in the garage in case of an emergency, a breakdown in the banking system, or the advertised coming economic collapse. Put faith into the cupboard just in case you need it.

By defining faith as "being fully persuaded" we realize that we cannot stockpile it. Faith is a state of being that we subjectively experience *in the moment.* Once the moment is gone there is another moment that calls for faith. Whether we were in the state of being fully persuaded in the moment before has no bearing on the present. Consider the example of Peter in Matthew. Jesus had just fed the five thousand and had sent the disciples on ahead while he went off to be alone. The disciples were in the boat struggling against the waves when Jesus came to them walking on water. The disciples feared it was a ghost:

> Jesus spoke to them saying, 'Take courage, it is I; do not be afraid.' And Peter answered Him and said, 'Lord, if it is You, command me to come to You on the water.' And he said, 'Come!' And Peter got out of the boat, and walked on the water and came toward Jesus. But seeing the wind, he became afraid, and beginning to sink, he cried out, saying, 'Lord, save me!' And immediately Jesus stretched out His hand and took hold of him, and said to him, 'O you of little faith, why did you doubt?' (Matthew 14:28-31)

Peter was fully persuaded that if Jesus commanded him to come, that he would be able to walk on the water. His faith even lasted for the first several steps out of the boat. It was not until he saw the wind whipping up the waves that he faltered. That Peter was fully persuaded moments before had no bearing on what happened in the next instant. Peter's persuasion changed from faith in Jesus' words to the circumstances—the raging storm and sea (though walking on glassy water does not seem any easier!). After Jesus grabbed and supported him, he said to Peter, "O you of little faith, why did you doubt?" The Greek definitions of both the words "little faith" and "doubt" are worth exploring.

The English phrase "of little faith" is the translation of the Greek word *oligopistos*, which itself is composed of *pistis* and *oligos*, meaning "small" or "little." However, the smallness is not of quantity, but of power. Perhaps the best way to reveal this is to consider a similar compound word in Greek, *oligopsuchos*, formed from *oligos* and *psuchos*, which means "soul" or "mind"; *oligopsuchos* is defined as "fainthearted," "fretful," "worried." We know that mind or soul are not quantities, so that small qualifies the power of the mind, not the size. Likewise, with faith the smallness refers to the degree of our persuasion.

The word "doubt" is the Greek word *distasis*. This word is formed from two Greek words *dis-*, "twice," "two ways" and *stasis*, "stand." It is defined as:

> To doubt, waver, hesitate, be uncertain . . . . It is a figurative word taken either from a person standing where two ways meet and not knowing which to choose (inclining sometimes to one, sometimes to the other), or from the quivering motion of a balance when the weights on either side are approximately equal (when first one side, then the other, seems to be predominant.)[43]

Doubting is standing unpersuaded, being unconvinced.

So then, we understand better what Jesus meant when he said to Peter, "O you of little faith, why did you doubt?" It is as if he were saying to Peter, "I have given you a 250-watt bulb with a dimmer switch—why did you hesitate and wonder whether your bulb would shine bright enough, when you yourself set it so low?"

---

[43]Ibid., 472.

This is the process that Jesus leads us through—to find the point at which we waver and hesitate. Hebrews 11:6 says that "without faith it is impossible to please [God]." But do not think then that it is bad to doubt! This is the exact opposite of what is true and helpful. We MUST find the point of doubt, the point of hesitancy. For this point of doubt—of not being fully persuaded—is also the point at which we believe that God will not defend us, where He will leave us alone to fend for ourselves. It is also the point at which, if we become afraid and begin to sink, He will reach out His hand and take hold of us, when we cry out to Him. Afterwards, when God has a firm hold of us, he asks us to examine why we hesitated. In this examination we discover the confidence to go farther the next time before we falter and hesitate. Like any good coach, Jesus presses us to just beyond the breaking point in order to take us to the next level. Be glad when you are pressed to the point of doubting, for you know that next time you will be fully persuaded that much longer. Some might call this position the point of failure, but from this failure springs a new crop of faith.

Faith that God Will Provide

We can find provision in only two places. We can believe that God will provide or we can believe that the circumstances will provide. The first looks to the internal condition of the heart. This reliance on God feeds the soul and is the pearl of great price. The victor guards this faith in his heart, protecting it not from external threats, but the internal threats of envy, greed, lust—all the manifold expressions of idolatry.

The internal relationship of believing for eternal life with God provides the context for hope and vision. As the Hebrews passage indicated, "Faith is the assurance of *things hoped for*"

(Hebrews 11:2, italics added). The living hope of eternal life is the evidence of Christ in us. When we carry that certainty within us, we are freed to pursue the highest calling we can imagine. Self-protection and the hedging of bets goes out the window, because our provision is in Christ's work as the author and finisher of our faith. When we rely on Jesus to be the Savior, we need no longer try to be our own savior. In contrast, when we attempt to save ourselves, we allow fear to reign in our hearts. Living to save ourselves from pain and humiliation prevents us from loving our neighbors as ourselves.

If we do not find the source of our provision in God, then it is in the circumstances. Remember Joshua and the other spies? The spies bringing the bad report looked only *at*, and therefore trusted *in*, circumstances. If we flag in our faith in God to provide, we invariably defer our hope, which the Scripture says makes the heart grow sick (Proverbs 13:12). Deferring hope means to put it outside of ourselves, i.e. in our circumstances. In his book *Sickness unto Death*, Søren Kierkegaard identified this sickness of heart as despair. Not that we literally die from despair, but despair results from the mistaken belief that we will change if our circumstances change.

When I (Derek) was first out of school, I wanted to serve God, but I didn't know how. I became involved with a dynamic church that had a school for ministry and a vision for our surrounding community. I counted on the church to fulfill my desire for ministering. I thought that the church leadership would direct me in some way or that I would receive a blessing which would enable me to minister. My thinking was quite naive. I thought that I wouldn't have to struggle to "work out my own salvation in fear and trembling" (Philippians 2:12). I wanted a magical experience that would release the passion of my heart and thus catapult me into a powerful ministry; something that would change me from the outside in. By placing my hope in the church leadership, I invited despair and death: my experience of church became stale and lifeless—a living death. It was only in deciding to pursue the dream in *my* own heart—experiencing a transformation from the inside out—that I returned to a passionate experience of life and relationship with God.

Love is the Fulfillment of Righteousness

In *love*, we come to the end of all theological discussions and intellectual diversions, the summation of all the Law and the Prophets, and the goal of all teaching, doctrine, study, and prayers. In love, we regard others before ourselves. We relate rightly—the way we all are created to live—when we love our neighbor as ourselves. Our love for our neighbor is also the measure of our love for God. John wrote,

> If someone says, "I love God," and hates his brother, he is a liar; for the one who does not love his brother whom he has seen, cannot love God whom he has not seen. (I John 4:20)

Love is the greatest of all—greater than faith and hope, because love is eternal. Faith and hope will pass away when God throws the last enemy, death, into the lake of fire (Revelation 20:14) and makes all things new, but love will remain forever.

The Scripture calls us to "love one another not in word only, but also in deed and in truth" (I John 3:18). A close look at these words in Greek reveals the difference between loving as a victim and loving as a victor. The word here for "word" is the Greek term *logos*—this suggests that our loving others is much more than talking about it. It is different than loving as a concept or an idea, as the textualist does. It is not based on some special revelation as a gnostic might believe. We are to love in deed and in truth. The word deed is translated from the Greek word *ergon* meaning "toil" and "struggle." This scripture here tells us that to love is a struggle, requiring a willingness to toil whether or not we are getting what we want from the one we are loving. This is why the victim refuses this kind of loving but rather looks for a way to justify being conditional in loving others. The word "truth" is *aletheia* which suggests that not only is there toil in loving others, but that in our loving we are to be true. That we are to love truthfully, in honesty, being faithful, in reality. This requires vision and commitment.

In giving His Son to live and die as a ransom in our place, God demonstrated His love for us. Jesus demonstrated righteousness by giving Himself as a ransom for the future He saw. The gift of Himself was the moment-by-moment fulfillment of the promises He explicitly and implicitly made. To be like Him, we must follow his example of making ourselves a ransom for our vision of the future.

8. The Struggle to Love

We know that we have passed out of death into life, because we love the brethren. He who does not love abides in death.

I John 3:14

God's design for the human race from the beginning has been to form a community of love—women and men bound by their love for God and each other. This is the aim of the Two Commandments and was expressed by Paul, who prayed that our "hearts may be encouraged, having been knit together in love, and attaining to all the wealth that comes from the full assurance of understanding, resulting in a true knowledge of God's mystery, that is, Christ Himself, in whom are hidden all the treasures of wisdom and knowledge" (Colossians 2:1-2). The Scriptures calls this community by various names: the household of God (I Timothy 3:15), the body (I Corinthians 10:17), a people of His own possession (Titus 2:14). Community, however, does not just happen; it requires diligent effort and meticulous maintenance.

However, unlike gardening, the care and growth of community does not respond to the simple rules of horticulture the way a garden does. Community does not come with Care and Feeding instructions: "For a vibrant community, plant "community seed" under 3 inches of soil, water every two days for 20 minutes; crop will mature in six to eight weeks."

So although we present in this chapter the necessary disciplines of life needed to form a community of love, there are no simple "how-to's" that work all the time, every time. Rather than static seeds that respond the same way to the same conditions, humans are dynamic. We "happen." In one moment, we respond one way, the next moment, in the same environment, we have different responses. The old idea that humans are "stimulus-response" machines, just doesn't hold up in real life.

Community requires us to be alert and open and flexible; watching closely the impact we make on others each moment. Running on autopilot does not work in nurturing God's community of love, neither does living as a victim. Both spell the death of community. Successful community requires not just loving others, but loving them in such a way that they *experience* the love you have for them. *This* is the struggle to love.

Only when we love others as we love ourselves, will they receive our love. If we are loving them *in order to* love ourselves; or if we are loving them *after* we love ourselves; or if we take any other relationship toward others, the love we feel will not reach them.

God's community has room for all, but only those who choose to be victors will walk in the liberty that Jesus has won for them on the cross. In contrast to the abundant life that Christ promised (John 10:10), the victim lives in constant suspicion that God will not provide for her and also may even take away what she already has. The victim suspects God foremost, but the suspicion flows downhill: all others are suspect as well. Thus the victim's experience of life is like walking through the abundance of heaven, all the while looking over her shoulder fearing disappointment, spending so much time and energy watching for someone out to get her, that she misses the magnificent beauty and provision of the kingdom of God.

Suspicion is a fruit of bitterness. Suspicion lays a charge on another based on little or no external evidence. Suspicion sees the similarity between those around us and those that hurt us in the past. Based on the bitterness and refusal to forgive someone for a prior wrong, the victim suspects the person presently in front of her.

Victims have no peace. Behind every bush someone may be lurking to hurt them again. The fear of abandonment and betrayal constantly haunt them. They greet even love, the very glue of the community, with suspicion. Every gift is carefully examined for the strings attached. And whenever a string is found—even in a loving community no motive is absolutely pure—the victim proves to himself once again that love, and every other human connection, is a signal to withdraw, withhold himself, and defend.

The victim's defense takes many forms. The common root in all defense is suspicion. The leaves and branches may be as different as a maple and a willow, but the root always is suspicion. Suspicion may appear as cynicism, sarcasm, ridicule, self-pity, or depression. Any act of love or generosity is held suspect: "Why is this person doing this for me?" "What do they want from me?" "Are they stupid? I don't deserve this." "If they really knew me they would never act this way." Such statements reek of unforgiveness held against others for what was done to us—for betrayal, for abandonment, for disappointment and hurt.

Suspicion is a thick taproot that dives deep into the soil of bitterness. Suspicion drives us from the life of community, and bitterness nurtures suspicion. The writer of Hebrews warns against the power of bitterness:

Make every effort to live in peace with all men and to be holy; without holiness no one will see the Lord. See to it that no one misses the grace of God and that no bitter root grows up to cause trouble and defile many. See that no one is sexually immoral, or is godless like Esau, who for a single meal sold his inheritance rights as the oldest son. (Hebrews 12:14-16, NIV)

Bitterness causes one to "come short of the grace of God." In this passage, the word "defile" means "to stain with color as the staining of glass; to tinge, pollute, defile."[44]

Bitterness takes our hurt and betrayal—any wrong done to us—and projects that out into all our relationships. Bitterness colors everyone with the hurt we live in. When we harbor bitterness we *cannot* love our neighbor as ourselves. Thus we fall short of the grace of God. His grace is available to all—He causes the rain to fall on the just and the unjust (Matthew 5:44-45). In falling short of the grace of God, we become profane, like Esau, who loved physical comfort more than his eternal inheritance.

The Life of Community

Our love not only glues the community together, it is the source of life. As the verse from I John 3:14 indicates, without love, we abide in death. Without love, our relationships become stale and lifeless. The true love of a Christian is not exclusively reserved for others in the community. Christ loves all—without exception. This is the standard that we are called

---

[44]Ibid., 984.

to live. Achieving this love, which is at once specific and universal, requires us to be and remain responsible.

Francis Frangipane writes:

> Is your love growing and becoming softer, brighter, more daring, and more visible? Or is it becoming more discriminating, more calculating, less vulnerable and less available? This is a very important issue, for your Christianity is only as real as your love is.[45]

Demonstrating love involves the making and keeping of promises. As we have seen in earlier chapters, the promises we make to others and the ones others make to us show tangibly the love that we share. However, the love is much more than the promises—the promises are containers of the love that flows from our hearts, as the sentiment of a poem is much more than the individual letters.

The challenge of being a victor is keeping our love fresh and new. In the moment, if we depend on our promises themselves to do the work of loving, we fall into victimhood once again. Having the letter of love without the spirit of love leads to "cold love." Jesus clearly outlined the reason for this in Matthew 24:12 when He said, "because lawlessness is increased, most people's love will grow cold." On the personal level, lawlessness is breaking our promises. On the social level, it is breaking the law collectively agreed upon which define civil order. On a spiritual level, it is violating the commandments God set forth for human beings to live a life of health and order.

We rarely use the word "lawlessness" in the modern vernacular; the best approximation is "criminal." The danger

---

[45]Francis Frangipane, *The Three Battlegrounds*, 49.

of using the word "criminal" is that it connotes an action worthy of arrest and possible confinement. Still, in God's eyes, we are all criminals, and act criminally whenever we relate as a victim. In another book we will examine the parallel strategies of the victim and the criminal. Interrupting lawlessness requires the responsible stand of a victor, which calls him to be a ransom.

Being a Ransom

In our culture, we use the word "ransom" to refer to the money paid to a kidnapper for the life of a hostage. In the widest sense of the word, "ransom" is the price paid for the life of another. In ancient times, it was a common practice for two warring kings who wanted peace to exchange hostages. The kings would exchange a son or daughter, or perhaps a niece or nephew, to live at each other's court. The hostages were the ransom or guarantee for the peace—they put their lives at risk in order to maintain the peace.

In practice, we become a ransom every time we bind ourselves to others in the making of a promise. It is in the act of making ourselves a ransom for another that we encounter the humiliation of taking up our cross daily and identify ourselves with Jesus, who is the ransom for whoever believes in Him.

Being a ransom demands everything that we are; there are no part-time ransoms. This sacrifice can take any form, it is not strictly giving up our physical life. We lay down our life whenever we relate responsibly—whenever we value our promise to another above our own convenience and desires, whenever we put our reputation and good name at stake for our promise. We also lay down our lives by being willing, whenever we fail to keep our promise to account for it. Being a ransom is the work of divine love.

The goal of being a ransom is to establish peace in our relationships, the true peace that is the fruit of reconciliation. This peace is not so much a state of tranquility as it is a state of safety from the attack of enemies; a poetic translation of "peace" from the Hebrew would read "having your knee on your enemy's neck!" This is a far cry from the victim's desire for peace at any cost. It is distinct from capitulation and is essential to building genuine community.

Once we build community, we must maintain it. This requires accountability—the willingness to give an account for our actions in relation to the explicit and implicit promises we have made. We practice the disciplines of community in one of these three domains of relationship: our relationships with others, others with us, and others with others. In this last case, one might argue that we are not a party to the relationships others have with third parties. Although we are not *directly* involved, we are the witnesses to these relationships and, as such, give our tacit consent to what transpires. Paul addresses this issue in I Corinthians 5:1, in which the Corinthian church was doing nothing to interrupt the incestuous immorality going on in their midst.

The Discipline of Accounting

The struggle of maintaining community lies in accounting for our broken promises. Indeed, it is through our broken promises that we see most clearly where we are headed in our life with God. Our broken promises show us the territory that we need to conquer if we would be transformed into His image.

Consider your own broken promises to others. Each one strains or even severs your bond with the one you promised. You either have worked to restore your relationship or have left it to languish in disrepair. The differences in the degree of restoration are due to the differences in the depth of your accounting. Restoration always begins with our accounting with others.

Who do you avoid because you broke a promise to them? Which broken promises do you refuse to face? Which ones are painful to talk about with the one you promised? To whom are you willing and eager to account for what was missing? Take a moment to list 10 broken promises. Think of the people you let down. What is common about them? What does this reveal about you and your relationships?

A broken promise tells us that *how* we sent ourselves was ineffective. Too often we use the circumstances to justify not keeping a promise. My favorite is traffic. "Traffic held me up," we say, whether it was true or not, whenever we are late for an appointment. It just rolls off our tongue. But what if $1 million were riding on being on time? How many of us would be late? Or would we find a way to circumnavigate every obstacle, even traffic? Whenever we are late or break any promise, we say that something was more important to us than the one to whom we promised.

Being on time and taking all measures to get where we've promised to be shows that we value what is at stake—the vision of the future our promise represents. Whenever we fail to keep a promise, it is because we have lost sight of our vision and have succumbed to the lure of the immediate relief that breaking the promise offers. God identified this surrender to our appetites as godless and evil: "that there be no immoral or godless person like Esau, who sold his own birthright for a single meal."

Maybe you think being on time or keeping "small" promises is nitpicky. But Jesus said, "He who is faithful in a very little thing is faithful also in much; and he who is unrighteous in a very little thing is unrighteous also in much" (Luke 16:10).

The good news is that we need not wait for some important moment to begin our transformation. As we remain faithful to our everyday relationships, we are sowing a future of abundance and grace. When I disregard the little things, like being on time, this small unrighteousness breeds gross sin.

Selfishness is first revealed in the little things of life. For example, my (Dan's) primary motive for marrying Aileen was her beauty and youth. I was with her to serve myself. I loved her because she liked the food I liked; she liked the movies I liked; she liked the people I liked. She made me feel good, look good and feel right. My wife was a tool to serve my own selfish idols.

As time went on in our life together I began to take her for granted. I began breaking small promises—things like being on time for dinner, going out or doing things around the house. Each time I broke a promise, it was because I wanted to do things I believed were more important. At first these things were activities like playing golf a little longer, playing chess a little longer, staying at work longer. Nothing that was grossly selfish—except in my wife's eyes! Whenever Aileen pointed out my insensitivity, I became indignant—after all, I was working hard so I needed to relax.

The more she tried to get my attention, the more I thought she did not understand me. I began to be offended and grew angry with her. Small broken promises multiplied into an all-consuming drug addiction and then into several adulterous relationships.

My self-centeredness knew no bounds. I had a rationale for every sin; I had a story that made me right about my selfishness. I rationalized the drugs as the only way I got to take time from my demanding schedule. I was in a high-pressure career; I made great money, I deserved an outlet. Besides, drugs helped me work longer hours. I rationalized my adultery in a couple of evil ways. I blamed my wife, of course. Aileen did not understand me and was intolerant of my need for recreational time. Besides, I only did it once in a great while. Surely what she did not know would not hurt her! After all I loved her; my liaisons were short-lived. Nobody would find out.

I had completely sold my inheritance and became godless like Esau. Each of these rationalizations was a victim story and all the victim stories supported each other. Bitterness and unforgiveness lay at the bottom of all of it. My parents, my teachers, my friends had all cheated me. I needed to take care of myself, because no one else was, including God.

Periodically I resolved to clean up my act, but nothing changed. It wasn't until I nearly lost Aileen and Danny that I went to the altar—confessing to Aileen and asking her for forgiveness. When I did, Aileen asked me gut-wrenching questions. She asked me, "Dan, when did it all start?" She was not interested in the deeds themselves as much as the attitude that was governing me. She pressed me to account for the *source* of my sin.

As I thought about it, I saw that I had been living this way a long time; long before I met her. Even as a small child, I remember thinking that I deserved something from others. I rationalized selfish deeds as what I needed to do to protect myself.

As a boy I became angry when my brother Corey was born because my father paid more attention to him than me. I thought that my dad did not love me and I used that as an excuse to do mean things to Corey. I'd wait until he was asleep, then punch him in the solar plexus. Of course, he would cry and my father would come and discipline me. I guess negative attention was better than no attention at all. I also hid Corey's toys and played rough with him. I made sure I gave him a few extra bumps and bruises. These "little" acts of unrighteousness developed into a pattern of criminal thinking that ultimately led to the selfish betrayals that threatened the inheritance I had with my wife and newborn son.

I unraveled these evil thought patterns in accounting with my wife. Once I recognized them, the difficult work of loving others began for me—the work of becoming a ransom for others. The work of redeeming the long string of broken promises that anchored me to the past and caused me to act out my victimhood in the present.

Whenever we break a promise, responsibility calls us to look at what was missing. How did we ransom ourselves for the one to whom we bound ourselves in our promise? For as Christians, with God as our Provider, all things are possible, including keeping our promises. Our deficiency is never in ability, but in our willingness to put everything we are into transforming our promises into realities. A broken promise always reveals the areas in which we do not believe that God will provide.

In our culture, we have turned accounting for our broken promises into simply a recounting of what occurred—a history lesson. This is not "confessing our faults one to another," it is just an admission of guilt. Confession requires not only an admission of the act or sin, but also an accounting for why I did what I did and the attitudes that prompted my actions.

Admission is often a great place to start the accounting process, but we must require more of ourselves if we want different results the next time a similar situation arises. We must be willing to examine how we are relating to people, how we are judging them.

This is the battleground in the struggle to love: do I choose to be true to others by sharing the dark motivations and blackness of my heart or do I excuse my actions? One of the questions that has assisted me in my struggle to love is: Am I relating to this person in the way I would have them relate to me? If in the accounting we do not identify what is missing in how we are giving ourselves, our accounting is incomplete. Rather than telling a story, accounting is directed to the future. Breaking a promise is evidence that our commitment is calling us to give ourselves in a different, complete way.

If we do not make a habit of counting the cost of relating as victims, we court the death of relationship with others. It is deeply disturbing to account for the specific details of our actions, because it breaks through the numbness we have felt towards others.

Private Accounting

Accounting for our actions in light of our vision is above all a private event. My request of others "to hold me accountable" gives the false impression that accountability is something another holds me to. Without my own determination, every external invitation to account is doomed to failure. Even if I go through the motions of accounting, without a heart that is willing to consider the prices others pay for our actions, no transformation is possible.

Even though accounting is a private event, I need someone else to hear my account. Why this is so is a mystery. In a perfect world, perhaps accounting to myself would be sufficient. But accounting while looking someone else in the eyes checks the temptation to dishonesty. Someone engaged in inquiring of me spurs questions that I may not have had the courage to ask myself.

My heart is not only the ground I must plow in order to account effectively. I must till the soil of my relationships for my vision to be realized. In fact, when I account I build a bridge to the future I know is possible, starting with a change of heart—a true repentance.

The depth of my accounting determines the depth of my repentance. The evidence of a sincere accounting is the willingness to expose both the specific transgression as well as the iniquity that is the source of the transgression. Any unwillingness to account is evidence that I am attempting to save myself. When I save myself, I have no need for Jesus Christ to be my savior.

Christian and non-Christians alike tend to want to save ourselves. When we are unwilling to recognize and expose our sin, we become our own saviors, saving ourselves from whatever consequence we fear from our sin.

Admitting sin is not synonymous with accounting. True accounting leads to an authentic repentance. The difference between admitting and authentic accounting is the degree of exposure of the heart. Norman Grubb compared Saul and David's repentance in this way:

> But let us note that the key to the reality of the whole of the Scriptures is the openness of the men of the Bible. We know of God's most intimate dealings with them, their sins and failures every bit as much as their successes. How do we know the details of Abraham's false step with Hagar, of Jacob's tricks with Isaac and Esau, of Moses' private act of disobedience concerning speaking to the rock? Of Elijah's flight and God's secret rebuke, of the inner history of Jonah? How did the disciples know the inside story of Jesus' temptations to record for us? Only because they were all open before their contemporaries. They lived in the light with each other as with God.

All through history men have turned in their fears and sorrows and doubts to the Psalms. Why? Because they are the heart experience of men in fear, and doubt, and guilt, and soul-hunger, describing how they had felt and how God had met them. Why was David's repentance acceptable to God and yet Saul's for a much less apparently carnal sin of failing to slaughter all the Amalakites, unacceptable? The reason is plain. Both kings, when faced respectively by the accusing finger of the prophets Nathan and Samuel, admitted their guilt before God, and said, "I have sinned (I Sam. 15:24 and II Sam. 12:13) but Saul's repentance was demonstrated to be insincere because he desired that his sin be hidden from the people (I Sam. 15:30), whereas the proof of David's utter brokenness was that he told the whole world in Psalm 51 what a sinner he was and that his only hope was in God's mercy. Openness before man is the genuine proof of sincerity before God, even as righteousness before man, and love to man are the genuine proofs of righteousness before God, and love to God.[46]

Saul admitted his sin to Samuel on the most superficial level, and then in the next breath shifted the blame to the people—before whom he wanted Samuel to honor him. David on the other hand was willing for all to know the depravity of his heart. David's greatness was not inborn talent; it was his dependence on God. In accounting for his sin, David made himself vulnerable to the rejection of the people.

---

[46]Norman Grubb, *Continuous Revival*, 16.

David's vulnerability and dependence on God turned him from a victim into a victor. David had made himself a victim when he gave in to his lust for Bathsheba. God had not provided him with the right wife. Uriah certainly didn't deserve such a wife. Since God had deprived David, he had to provide for himself. In accounting and repenting openly—depending only on God—David defeated an enemy every bit as fierce and terrifying as Goliath.

For us as for David, every victory implies that we vanquish an enemy. As we take responsible action in pursuit of our visions, depending on God to guide us, we kill the victim. Regardless of whether we are Christian or not, the law of the universe is that responsible action kills the victim. Like David, we may progress from killing the lion and the bear to killing the giant Goliath, and finally even the victim within. But we are all victims to the last enemy: death.

Death is a curtain beyond which we cannot gaze. To date, it has claimed all that have lived except one: Jesus of Nazareth. We are victors over death only by being fully persuaded that Jesus himself bore the punishment for our sins. Nothing we do saves us: no action, however responsible; no matter how many promises we keep; no matter how humbly we live. Only God's grace received as a gift through faith defeats the last enemy.

Without Christ, death claims us. Death makes every one who has not believed in Jesus Christ into a victim. A woman or man who responds to the invitation to believe joins Jesus as a victor over death.

Unconquerable Love

Defeating any enemy is difficult—none of what we've outlined in the previous chapters comes easy. The apostle Paul describes his own struggle to "kill the victim within" in his letter to the Romans. In it he details the battle between sin and grace, death and life, slavery and freedom, the wages of sin and God's precious gift. He agonizes over the dichotomy between the new nature (read: Christ) and the old (read: victim) nature that was crucified with Christ but still rears its ugly head whenever we let down on our commitment to love as Christ loved. The great apostle himself fought daily against his sin victim nature and wrote passionately about it in his letter to the Romans. Note how well he describes the subtlety of the victim within us. The victim is sly. He creeps in on cat's paws and cools the love in our hearts. We drift away from those we love and begin to set our heart on other things. We place an idol on the throne instead of God. Paul saw this dilemma all too clearly in Romans 7:15-25:

> What I don't understand about myself is that I decide one way, but then I act another, doing things I absolutely despise. So if I can't be trusted to figure out what is best for myself and then do it, it become obvious that God's command is necessary.
>
> But I need something more! For if I know the law but still can't keep it, and if the power of sin within me keeps sabotaging my best intentions, I obviously need help! I realize that I don't have what it takes. I can will it but I can't do it. I decide to do good, but I don't really do it; I decide not to do bad, but then I do it anyway. My decisions, such as they are, don't result in actions. Something has gone wrong deep within me and gets the better of me every time. It happens so regularly that it's predictable. The moment I decide to do good, sin is there to trip me up. I

truly delight in God's commands, but it's pretty obvious that not all of me joins in that delight . . . I'm at the end of my rope. Is there no one who can do anything for me? . . . the answer, thank God, is that Jesus Christ can and does.[47]

Of course the answer lies in Christ and His ability, not in our own power. It is He who makes the greatest promise of all—that of eternal life and fellowship with the Lord God Almighty. It is He who gives us the power to overcome and kill the victim within. Throughout the letter to the Romans, Paul encourages us to crucify the old man, the old sin nature, the victim—if you will—and turn toward a life of promise and fulfillment.

David is an example of the power of unconquerable love. His love for others was revealed in Psalm 51—he held nothing back from others. He gave everything for others, even his own dark sin. Because he loved in this way, Paul called him "a man after God's own heart" (Acts 13:22).

The love of God is unconquerable. No matter what the situation and circumstances are, no one and nothing can separate us from the love of God. Paul wrote in Romans:

What then shall we say to these things? If God is for us, who is against us? He who did not spare His own Son, but delivered Him up for us all, how will He not also with Him freely give us all things? Who will bring a charge against God's elect? God is the one who justifies; who is the one who condemns? Christ Jesus is He who died, yes, rather who was raised, who is at the right hand of God, who also intercedes for us. Who shall separate us from the love of Christ? Shall tribulation, or distress, or persecution, or

---

[47]Romans 7:15-25 from *The Message* by Eugene Peterson.

famine, or nakedness, or peril, or sword? Just as it is written, "For Thy sake we are being put to death all day long; we were considered as sheep to be slaughtered." But in all these things we overwhelmingly conquer through Him who loved us. For I am convinced that neither death, nor life, nor angels, nor principalities, nor things present, nor things to come, nor powers, nor height, nor depth, nor any other created thing, shall be able to separate us from the love of God, which is in Christ Jesus our Lord. (Romans 8:31-39)

Not only are we inseparable from God's love for us, but God's love in us is equally unconquerable. What makes both God's love and our love unconquerable is our willingness to die for others—not so much in a glorious physical martyrdom—but daily in the suffering of rejection, persecution, shame, guilt, suspicion, and humiliation. This is what Paul meant by "for your sake we are being put to death all day long."

What continually dies in us is the victim! The victim must die a thousand deaths, then another and another. The victim must be continually put on the altar or we will drift away from those we love and begin to set our hearts on other *things*. We will put an idol on the throne instead of God.

In place of the love, the victim finds a cold knot of fear. It is at the point of fear that our love fails and we surrender the unconquerable love of God in our hearts. There is no victory in fear. What victory is there in fearing to talk with someone who wears crystals and believes in the mystical power of pyramids? What victory is there if we shun anyone who speaks differently, acts differently, or believes differently? If we fear being overrun by evil, we have already made ourselves a hostage to the enemy. Only by facing fear will we plumb the depths of God's unconquerable love. Wherever fear reigns, love suffers defeat.

Only in living as Jesus lived—God's example of a life of unconquerable love—do we have hope for lasting victory over the victim within. Jesus did what few Christians would do today: He ate, drank, and talked with the sordid people of His day. He loved without condition. Jesus reveals that no strategy, no tactic, no program transforms us. Nothing but love is unconquerable. Only love remains.

Appendix

Orthodoxy is literally "right teaching." Mashiyach aligns with Christian orthodoxy by adhering to the following four creeds.

The Apostles' Creed

I believe in God, the Father almighty, maker of heaven and earth;

And in Christ Jesus his only Son, our Lord; who was conceived of the Holy Ghost, born of the Virgin Mary, suffered under Pontius Pilate, was crucified, dead, and buried. He descended into hell. The third day he rose again from the dead. He ascended into heaven, and sitteth on the right hand of God the Father almighty. From thence he shall come to judge the quick and the dead.

I believe in the Holy Ghost, the holy catholic church, the communion of saints, the forgiveness of sins, the resurrection of the body, and the life everlasting. Amen.

Nicene Creed

We believe in one God, the Father, the Almighty, maker of heaven and earth, of all that is, seen and unseen.

We believe in one Lord, Jesus Christ, the only son of God, eternally begotten of the Father, God from God, Light from Light, true God from true God, begotten, not made, of one

Being with the Father. Through him all things were made. For us and for our salvation he came down from heaven: by the power of the Holy Ghost he became incarnate from the Virgin Mary, and was made man. For our sake he was crucified under Pontius Pilate; he suffered death and was buried. On the third day he rose again in accordance with the Scriptures; he ascended into heaven and is seated at the right hand of the Father. He will come again in glory to judge the living and the dead, and his kingdom will have no end.

We believe in the Holy Ghost, the Lord, the giver of life, who proceeds from the Father [and the Son]. With the Father and the Son he is worshiped and glorified. He has spoken through the Prophets. We believe in one holy catholic and apostolic Church. We acknowledge one baptism for the forgiveness of sins. We look for the resurrection of the dead, and the life of the world to come. Amen.

The Athanasian Creed

Whosoever will be saved, before all things it is necessary that he hold the Catholic Faith. Which Faith except everyone do keep whole and undefiled, without doubt he will perish everlastingly. And the Catholic faith is this: That we worship One God in Trinity and Trinity in Unity, neither confounding the Persons, nor dividing the Substance. For there is one Person of the Father, another of the Son, another of the Holy Ghost. But the Godhead of the Father, of the Son, and of the Holy Ghost, is all one, the Glory equal, the Majesty co-eternal. Such as the Father is, such is the Son, and such is the Holy Ghost. The Father uncreate, the Son uncreate, and the Holy Spirit uncreate. The Father incomprehensible, the Son incomprehensible, the Holy Ghost incomprehensible. The Father eternal, the Son eternal, and the Holy Ghost eternal. And yet they are not three eternals but one eternal. As also there are not three incomprehensibles, nor three uncreated, but one uncreated, and one incomprehensible. So likewise the Father is Almighty, the Son Almighty, and the Holy Ghost Almighty.

And yet they are not three Almighties but one Almighty. So the Father is God, the Son God, and the Holy Ghost is God. And yet they are not three Gods, but one God. So likewise the Father is Lord, the Son Lord, and the Holy Ghost Lord. And yet not three Lords, but one Lord. For like as we are compelled by the Christian verity to acknowledge every Person by himself to be both God and Lord, So are we forbidden by the Catholic Religion, to say, There be three Gods, or three Lords. The Father is made of none, neither created nor begotten. The Son is of the Father alone, not made, nor created, but begotten. The Holy Ghost is of the Father and of the Son, neither made, nor created, nor begotten, but proceeding. So there is one Father, not three Fathers; one Son, not three Sons; one Holy Ghost, not three Holy Ghosts. And in this Trinity none is afore, or after other; none is greater, or less than another; But the whole three Persons are co-eternal together and co-equal. So that in all things, as is aforesaid, the Unity in Trinity and the Trinity in Unity is to be worshiped. He therefore that will be saved must thus think of the Trinity.

Furthermore, it is necessary to everlasting salvation that he also believe rightly the Incarnation of our Lord Jesus Christ. For the right Faith is, that we believe and confess, that our Lord Jesus Christ, the Son of God, is God and Man; God, of the Substance of the Father, begotten before the worlds; and Man, of the Substance of his Mother, born in the world; Perfect God and perfect Man, of a reasonable soul and human flesh subsisting; Equal to the Father, as touching His Godhead; and inferior to the Father, as touching his Manhood. Who although he be God and Man, yet he is not two, but one Christ; One, not by conversion of the Godhead into flesh, but by taking of the Manhood into God; One altogether; not by confusion of Substance, but by unity of Person. For as the reasonable soul and flesh is one man, so God and Man is one Christ; Who suffered for our salvation, descended into hell, rose again the third day from the dead. He ascended into heaven, he sitteth on the right hand of the Father, God Almighty, from whence he shall come to judge the quick and the dead. At whose coming all men shall rise again with their bodies and shall give account for their own works. And they that have done good shall go into life everlasting; and they that have done evil into everlasting fire. This is the Catholic Faith, which except a man believe faithfully, he cannot be saved.

Definition of Chalcedon

Therefore, following the holy fathers, we all with one accord teach men to acknowledge one and the same Son, our Lord Jesus Christ, at once complete in Godhead and complete in manhood, truly God and truly man, consisting also of a reasonable soul and body; of one substance (homoousios) with the Father as regards his Godhead, and at the same time of one substance with us as regards his manhood; like us in all respects, apart from sin; as regards his Godhead, begotten of the Father before the ages, but yet as regards his manhood begotten, for us men and for our salvation, of Mary the Virgin, the God-bearer (Theotokos); one and the same Christ, Son, Lord, Only-begotten, recognized in two natures, without confusion, without change, without division, without separation; the distinction of natures being in no way annulled by the union, but rather the characteristics of each nature being preserved and coming together to form one person and subsistence, not as parted or separated into two person, but one and the same Son and Only-begotten God the Word, Lord Jesus Christ; even as the prophets from earliest times spoke of him, and our Lord Jesus Christ himself taught us, and the creed of the Fathers has handed down to us.

Glossary

This glossary of terms contains many of the critical words and concepts for killing the victim. They are a combination of definitions from Noah Webster's original *American Dictionary of the English Language* and our own understanding.

Accountability (account, accountable): The state of being liable to answer for one's conduct; liability to give account.

Assertion: The act of stating or putting forward positively; affirmation. An assertion is an interpretation of reality that is backed up with evidence.

Authority: The power derived from opinion, respect, or esteem; influence of character or office; credit. Authority is not primarily a position, rather it is a relationship in which the authority has created value with others.

Breakdown: A situation or occurrence in which a broken promise, or a circumstance, threatens the keeping of a promise, or the fulfillment of a vision or commitment.

Breakthrough: The result of standing responsibly during a breakdown such that circumstances or people that previously had hindered the completion of a promise or commitment, now foster and aid its fulfillment.

Commitment (commit): The determination of will that is sent with a promise. The word commitment shares the same root word in Latin, *mittere*, as promise, and literally means "to send with."

Conscience: Internal or self-knowledge, or judgment of right and wrong; or the faculty, power, or principle within us, which decides on the lawfulness or unlawfulness of our *own* actions and affections, and instantly approves or condemns them.

Declaration (declare): The act of making known or announcing explicit commitments with authority and conviction. Declarations shape vision.

Grace: [Greek, *karis*] The free gift of God that results in relating to life, even its tragedies, with rejoicing and thankfulness. Theologians call this "unmerited favor."

Heart: A metaphor denoting the essence of our being; ourselves; our internal world of thoughts, emotions, and beliefs.

Mashiyach Ministries: A nonprofit company dedicated to the transformation of character. The heart of Mashiyach Ministries is reconciliation in the broadest sense: the establishment of peace in relationships where it has never been before, or to restore peace in relationships where it has been broken. Foremost is reconciliation between God and man, but also between individuals, in families, organizations, and among races and nations. Our mission takes form in the *Momentus*, *One Accord*, and *Legacy* programs.

Momentus: A four-day experiential learning environment that affords the opportunity for you to discover and realign the belief systems which govern your life, such that you experience a transformation in your ability to love others as Christ loves you, liberating your conscience to fulfill God's unique purposes for you with freedom, passion, and power.

Objective: Existing independent of mind; pertaining to an object as it is in itself or as distinguished from consciousness or the subject.

Performative language: An expression that serves to effect a transaction or that constitutes the performance of the specified act by virtue of its utterance. Performative language transforms reality. The pillars of performative language are declarations, assertions, and requests. Promises are a special form of declaration; ransoming another through your promise is a performative act.

Promise: [Latin, *pro*-, forward + *mittere*, to send, that is, to send forth] In a general sense, a declaration, written or verbal, made by one person to another, which binds the person who makes it either in honor, conscience, or law, to do or forbear a certain act specified; a declaration which gives the person to whom it is made, a right to expect or to claim the performance or forbearance of the act.

A promise creates an obligation. A complete promise includes a speaker, a listener, specific terms of fulfillment (exactly what will be produced), and a time agreement (by when).

Ransom: In the broadest sense, it is the price paid for the life of another, e.g., the money paid to a kidnapper for the life of a hostage. Being a ransom demands everything that we are; there are no part-time ransoms. Being a ransom is the work of divine love.

Reconciliation: Restoration of peace in relationships where it has been broken or the establishment of peace in relationships where it has never been.

Repentance: a total change of mind, heart, and purpose (*metanoia* in Greek) from loving self to loving others, from knowing truths to being true, from being a victim to being a victor.

Request: The act of asking for something. A complete request includes a speaker, a listener, specific terms of fulfillment (exactly what will be produced), a time agreement (by when), and a response (accept, decline, or counter offer).

Responsible (responsibility): derived from the Latin root, *respondere*, it means "to promise back." Responsible action defeats being a victim.

Revival: To revive, to come alive, or bring back from a coma or death. A period of awakening when God graciously breathes new life into His people. It is marked by an outpouring of the Holy Spirit which restores them to a heightened spiritual life after a period of individual and corporate decline.

Salvation: The state of being reconciled to God through faith in the death, resurrection, and ascension of Jesus Christ. Faith is received as a gift of grace, as indicated in Ephesians 2:8-9, "For by grace you have been saved through faith; and that not of yourselves, it is the gift of God; not as a result of works, that no one should boast."

Sanctification: The on-going process of being continually transformed into the image of Christ; this involves killing the victim.

Self-government: The God-given ability to direct one's thoughts, feelings, and actions toward the greatest good, with freedom, passion, and power. Self-control; one of the fruit of the Spirit.

Soul: In the Hebrew language, soul is distinguished by the two words *shem* and *nephesh*. *Shem* is used to designate the public self, while *nephesh* refers to the private self. In Greek philosophy, soul is composed of mind, emotions, and will, and is usually placed between spirit and body; as in spirit, soul, and body.

Subjective: Of, pertaining to, or determined by the mind, ego, or consciousness, as the subject of experience and knowledge; belonging to reality as perceived or known, as opposed to reality as independent of mind.

Submit: In the Bible, submit carries the sense of being fully persuaded (whether rightly or wrongly) to a point of view.

Transformation: The process of shifting the relationship taken to a person or event; such shifting occurs moment by moment and is not permanent.

Truth: Reality. The underlying essence of matter that is the basis of and agrees with the appearance.

Victim: a) One that is acted upon and usually adversely affected by a force or agent, or one that is injured, destroyed, or sacrificed under any of various conditions; b) A living being sacrificed to a deity or in a performance of a religious rite. Being a victim is a way of relating to people and events in which the individual surrenders control of his life to others.

Victor: One who stands firm on the promises of God and his own promises regardless of circumstances, because he is fully persuaded that all will turn out for the good to those who love God and are called according to His purposes (Romans 8:28).

Vision: Experiencing a future worth having in relationship with others. It requires a willingness to stand responsibly in the present with a focus on a future possibility coming into reality. Its structure is dynamic, open-ended, and generative.

Bibliography

Buber, Martin. *I and Thou.* New York: Scribner's, 1958; reprint ed. New York: Macmillian Publishing Company, 1987.

Cheney, Margaret. *Tesla: Man Out of Time.* New York: Dorset Press, 1981.

Frangipane, Francis. *The Three Battlegrounds.* Cedar Rapids: Advancing Church Publications, 1989.

Grubb, Norman. *Continuous Revival.* Fort Washington: Christian Liturature Crusade, 1996.

Jones, Alan. *Soul Making: the Desert Way of Spirituality.* New York: HarperCollins Publishers, 1985.

Keller, W. Phillip. *A Layman Looks at the Lamb of God.* Minneapolis: Bethany House Publishers, 1982.

Kierkegaard, Søren. *Works of Love.* Edited and translated by Howard V. Hong and Edna H. Hong. Princeton: Princeton University Press, 1995.

Lewis, C. S. *The Four Loves.* New York: Harcourt Brace Jovanovich, 1960.

Lewis, C. S. *The Weight of Glory and Other Addresses.* New York: Macmillian Publishing Company, 1949; revised and expanded, 1980.

McCullough, Donald W. *The Trivialization of God: The Dangerous Illusion of a Manageable Deity.* Colorado Springs: Navpress, 1995.

Peterson, Eugene H. *Psalms.* Colorado Springs: Navpress, 1994.

Peterson, Eugene H. *The Message.* Colorado Springs: Navpress, 1993.

Pieper, Joseph. *The Four Cardinal Virtues.* Notre Dame: University of Notre Dame Press, 1966.

Schlossberg, Herbert. *Idols for Destruction: Christian Faith and its Confrontation with American Society.* New York: Thomas Nelson Publishers, 1983.

Tozer, A.W. *Keys to the Deeper Life.* Grand Rapids: Zondervan Publishing House, 1957.

Vine, W.E. et al. *Vine's Complete Expository Dictionary of Old and New Testament Words.* Nashville: Thomas Nelson Publishers, 1985.

Webster, Noah. *An American Dictionary of the English Language.* New York: S. Converse, 1828; reprint ed. San Francisco: Foundation for American Christian Education, 1967.

Zodhiates, Spiros. *The Complete Word Study Dictionary: New Testament.* Chattanooga: AMG Publishers, 1992.

Index

A

Aaron, 153-154

abandonment, 205

abortion, 34

Abraham, 79

    expectation in God's promises, 107-108

    God's promises to, 80-81, 110-111

    sacrifice of Isaac, 71-74

accomplishments, 181

account, unwillingness to, 215

accountability, 45, 51- 52, 209, 212

    definition of, 227

    private/public, 214

    versus confession, 213

action

    prudent, definition of, 52

    taking, 25-26, 31

actions

    accounting for, 48

    heart's state manifested through, 48

    versus intentions, 49

Adam, 26-30, 102-103

addictions, 87, 112-113, 211-212

    drug, 67- 68

admiration, 125

admission, versus accountability, 213

admittance, 215

adultery, 211-212

alcoholism, 122

aletheia, 44

alternating current (AC), 90

anger, 22, 37, 93

Antichrist, nature of, 146

ants, habits of, 17

apathy, versus peace, 130

Apostles' Creed, 223

appearances, 162, 165, 172

    as idols, 137-138, 143

approval, as an idol, 144

Aquinas, Thomas, 52

    definition of justice, 123

Arameans, siege of Samaria, 94

arbitrary self-will, 117

arrogance, 93

    relationship to humiliation, 55- 57

Ashtaroth, 153

assertion, definition of, 227

assurance, 190

Athanasian Creed, 224-226

attention, need for, 213

authenticity, 142

authority

definition of, 227

to steward life, 24

faith in, 200

having peace in, 129

preventing vision, 167

relationship to vision, 49

seeing God's provision in, 50

sensationalizing, 159

yielding to, 32

civil government, relationship to self-government, 118

civil law, breaking, 207

cocaine, 112-113

cold fusion, 192

cold love, 207

comfort, 170

exchanging for vision, 180

loving, 206

need for, 17

securing, 43

commitment

as safeguard of reputation, 115

breakdowns in, 89

definition of, 111, 228

for reform, 36

relationship to promise, 51, 90-92, 111

responsibility to assess, 103-104

to vision, 114

communication, censoring, 142

Communism, 35

communities of love, 203-206, 209

community, God's principal of, 42

comparisons, unfavorable, 143

compass, who/what is in control as, 32

complacency, 43

compunction, 58-59

concentration camps, release from, 19

concepts as idols, 141

conditional love, 143

confession, 117, 138

of David, 216

of Saul, 216

versus accountability, 213

confidence, 190

conflict, form as source of, 171

confusion, 93

conscience, 96, 138

binding through, 95-96

definition of, 228

educating, 125

seared, 125

wakening, 126

consequences

of promise, 84

of textualism, 48

saving ourselves from, 215

constraint, through vision, 115

control, 157

as idol, 139

desire to, 50

knowing what we can, 56

mind, 160-161

of creation, 25

our attempts to, 88

revealed through breakdowns, 87

surrendering, 24

who/what is in, 16, 21-26, 32, 35

convenience, relating to God through, 120

conviction, 190

convictions as idols, 141, 142

E

eating, 37

Edison, Thomas, 90, 114

Edwards, Jonathan, 35

eidos, 162

elengkos, 190

emotions

    fluidity of, 96-97

    motivations of, 85

    understanding versus expressing, 140

enemies, vanquishing, 217, 218

entropy, 89

envy, 37, 188

ergon, 202

Esau, 180, 206, 210-212

eternal life, faith in, 200

Eve, 26- 30, 102-103

evil

    interpretations of reality, 43

    setting own standards of, 29

evil reports, believing over God, 42

evil speaking, forgiving, 124

exaggerating, 143

existentialism, 133

expectation, in promises, 109

expectations, created through promise, 107-108

explicit promises, 95

external versus internal, 184

external resources, dependence on, 19

extortion, 159

F

failure, 26

faith, 43, 189

    as proof of vision, 191

    as quantity, 196

    as subjective condition, 196

    as virtue, 52

    dying for, 160

    having little, 198

    in God's provision, 178, 199-200

    in promises, 109

    relationship with vision, 179

    strengthening, 125

    through promise, 110

faithfulness in small things, 211

false sincerity, 23

fantasies, 167

fault, 99

fear, 194-195, 220-221

    of deception, 186

feedback, 130, 193

feeling good, 169

feelings

    as determiners of action, 26

    communicated through action, 76

    demonstrating through promise, 85

feminism, militant, 35

filters of reality, 41

fleeces (Gideon's), 31

flesh, lust of, 170

flexibility, 131

focusing on self, 29

forgiveness, 18, 24, 122

    as release, 124

    derivation of, 121

    freedom through, 98

relationship to arrogance, 55-57

response to, 64

hupostasis, 190

hurt, 205

past dictating present, 26

hypnosis, 160

I

icons, societal, 139

identity

defining, 168

determining, 164

idolatrous relationships, 157, 158, 168

idolatry, 99, 137

as manifestation of unbelief, 158

as value system, 142

at Mount Sinai, 154

connection with greed, 170

definition of, 146, 162, 165

derivation of, 162

freedom stolen through, 146

in today's society, 152

interrupting, 166

of doctrine, 148

payoffs for, 172

relationship to appearances, 165

transformation because of, 177

versus promise, 151

idols, 171-172, 218

appearances as, 143

approval as, 144

as source of provision, 120

concepts as, 141

convictions as, 141-142

definition of, 88

dethroning of, 151

doctrines as, 148-150

form as, 140-141, 163

Israelites, 153

of control, 139

of image, 138-139

principles as, 141

rationality as, 139-142

revealed through lack of peace, 129

sacrifices to, 159

uncovering roots of, 143

what they are, 152

worshipping, 142

images, idolatry of, 138-139

implicit promises, 95-97

imprisonment, release from, 19

incest, 209

indifference, 110, 130, 133-134

influences, dangerous, 155

iniquities, forgiving, 124

iniquity, exposing, 215

injustices of life, 59

Inquisition, The, 161

intentions

proving through actions, 48

versus actions, 49

without promise, 92

internal versus external, 184

interpretations of reality, 41, 44

evil versus good, 43

intimacy, 104-105

building through promise, 92-93, 110

restoring, 128

mission statement, 228
master, 153
   reaction to broken promises, 109
   versus servant, 124
materialism, 35
maturity, 16
   through suffering, 57
McCullough, Donald W., 131-132
mercenaries, 165
Messiah, deliverance from tyranny, 33- 34
Messianic prophecies, fulfillment of, 84-85
metamorphoo, 174-175
metamorphosis, 175- 177
building blocks of, 178
metanoia, 18-19, 33, 113
metaschematizo, 174-177
method, scientific, 192
Midianites, 31
mind, change of, 18-19, 33
mind control, 160-161
ministry, Jesus' vision of, 19
miracles, waiting for, 166
molestation, 121
Momentus training, 16, 23, 57, 62, 79, 93,
   104-105, 140, 155-157, 193
   mission statement, 228
money, lust for, 170
Moses, 41, 46, 145, 153, 170
Mother Theresa, 17
Mount Moriah, 72- 73
Mount Sinai, 153-154

N

name of Jesus, 64-65

narcissism, 165
nature, new versus old, 218
Nazis, 133-134
necessity, 181
neighbors, loving
   as ourselves, 150, 201
   versus loving God, 149
nephesh, 96
   leaning on own, 102
New Age, 164
Nicene Creed, 223-224
Nine Dot Problem, 176
nominalizations, 178, 191
Nuremberg trials, 133

O

oaths
   definition of, 100
   distinction from promise, 101
   revealing lack of trust, 102
obedience
   through suffering, 57
   unconditional, 148-150
objective reality, 192-195
objectives, definition of, 229
objectivity, 192
   versus subjectivity, 184
obsession, 194
offense, as indication of irresponsibility,
   104
oligopistos, 198
oligopsuchos, 198
omnipotence of babies, 56
orientation of maps, 32

orthodoxy, definition of, 223

P

pain
  burying, 140
  short-term, 17
passion, 181, 188
  channeling into vision, 182
Paul, 127, 155-156, 218
  crucifying the old man, 219
  Damascus transformation, 177, 188
  hearts knit together, 203
paying one's dues, 59
payoffs of idolatry, 170-172
peace
  establishing through ransom, 209
  in relationships, 128
  regardless of circumstances, 129
  restoration of, 127
  versus apathy, 130
peitho, 191
penthos, 58
performance, 143
performative language, definition of, 229
persecution, 220
persuasion, 190-191, 197
Peter
  faith of, 197
  humiliation of, 60
  sifting of, 52
Peterson, Eugene, 65
Pharaoh, 145
Pharisees, 93
physical universe

feedback from, 130
reality of, 46
Pieper, Joseph, 123
pistis, 191
possibilities through promise, 124
possibility, 181
  despair of, 91, 182
power
  lust for, 170
  of choice, 24
practice versus doctrine, 48
praise, 125
prejudging, 142
presuppositions, 142
pride, 37, 188
principles
  as idols, 141
  of selfishness, 51
private accounting, 214
problems, one's response to, 37
promise
  as act of faith, 107-110
  as demonstration of feelings, 85
  as means of relating, 78-79
  as standard for behavior, 116
  binding through, 98
  bringing order to chaos, 89-90
  building intimacy through, 92- 93
  characteristics of, 132
  combined with vision, 91
  definition of, 229
  derivation of, 77, 121
  glorifying God through, 115
  relationship to

commitment, 90, 111

forgiveness, 121

responsibility, 99

revealing attitude of the heart, 86

twelve propositions of, 78-79

versus emotion, 97

versus idolatry, 151

Promised Land, spies sent to survey, 41-42

promises

accounting for broken, 92-93

adding oaths to, 100-102

as containers of love, 207

as ransom, 208

attitudes toward, 134

binding, 95

breaking, 82, 87

broken, 104, 210, 213

as territory to conquer, 209

forgiving, 123

impact of, 108

leading to repentance, 126

our attitude toward, 109

characteristics of, 117

declaring, 92

freedom to account for, 131

God's

as tool of revelation, 83

standing on, 88

to Abraham, 72-74, 80- 81

to Mary, 83-84

implicit/explicit, 94-97

making/keeping, 75-76, 172, 207

as possibilities for glory, 125

relating to God through, 120

relationship to commitment, 51

small, 125, 211

prophecies, Messianic, 84-85

prophecy, 83

prophetic visions, God as source of, 182

propositional truths, 46-48

protection, false, 183

provision

depending on, 120

faith in God's, 28, 199, 200

not trusting God for, 86

prudence as virtue, 52

prudent, definition of, 52

public accounting, 214

punctuality, 210-211

purpose

having sense of, 180

of freedom, 49

Q

quantity of faith, 196

quarrels, ending, 172

R

rage, 37, 188

ransom, 213

definition of, 127, 208, 229

giving of oneself as, 202

goal of, 209

rape, 34, 121

rationality as idol, 139-142

rationalizations, comfort of, 180

reality

testing God (Gideon's fleeces), 31

textualism, 47, 184-188

  consequences of, 48

theft, 34

thermodynamics, second law of, 89

thinking, cathedral, 39

thinness, lust for, 170

Thomas Aquinas, 52

toil, 202

toxic shame, 62

Tozer, A. W., 186

traditions, tyranny of, 33

traffic as excuse for broken promises, 210

tranquility, establishing through ransom, 209

transformation

  definition of, 231

  of character, 173-177

  of heart, 173-177

  test of, 113

transgressions

  exposing, 215

  forgiving, 124

tree of knowledge of good and evil, 27-30, 102

triangulation, 104

trust, 31, 120

  lack of, revealed through oaths, 102

  reestablishing after breakdown, 110

truth

  and reality, relationship of, 44

  definition of, 231

  knowing versus living the, 46-47

  loving in, 202

  propositional, 46-48

  tyranny of professed, 51

Twain, Mark, 90-91

tyranny, 32-33

  deliverance from, 34

  of professed truth, 51

tyrants, limits of, 37

U

unconditional love, 221

unconditional obedience, 150

undisciplined, 179

unforgiveness, 205, 212

  binding through, 98

universe, physical, 46

Uriah, 217

V

value, focusing on, 168

value systems, idolatry as, 142

victim, definition of, 27, 159, 231

victimhood

  as foundation for rebellion, 33

  manifestations of, 36

victims

  Adam and Eve as, 26-30

  response to problems, 37

  slavery of, 44

  subtlety of, 218

  to the Savior, 34

  victimizing others, 69

victor, definition of, 29

victors

  character traits of, 18-20

Order Form
Killing the Victim before the Victim Kills You

Establishing Responsible Relationships through Making and Keeping Promises

Fill in this form and then:

for mail orders, send form to: Mashiyach Press, 1055 W. College Avenue #286, Santa Rosa, CA 95401.

for fax order, fax form to: (707) 542-2382.

for phone orders, call: (707) 542-1053.

Name:_____

Address:_____

City:_____ State: _____ Zip:_____

Phone: (___) _____ Fax: (___) _____

Please send me _____ copies of Killing the Victim

$16.95 X _____ copies	$
Shipping: $3.50 for one book + $1 each additional book (Canada and Mexico pay 1.5X and international orders pay 2X shipping)	
CA Residents add 7.5% sales tax	
Total Payment in U.S. funds	$

❑ Check (Make checks payable to Mashiyach Press)
❑ Visa ❑ MasterCard ❑ AMEX
#_____

Expiration Date _____

Signature _____

Date_____

Visit our CyberNet-designed Web site: http://www.momentus.org/mash/

Order Form
Killing the Victim before the Victim Kills You

Establishing Responsible Relationships through Making and Keeping Promises

Fill in this form and then:

for mail orders, send form to: Mashiyach Press, 1055 W. College Avenue #286, Santa Rosa, CA 95401.

for fax order, fax form to: (707) 542-2382.

for phone orders, call: (707) 542-1053.

Name:_____

Address:_____

City:_____ State: _____ Zip:_____

Phone: (___) _____ Fax: (___) _____

Please send me _____ copies of Killing the Victim

$16.95 X _____ copies	$
Shipping: $3.50 for one book + $1 each additional book (Canada and Mexico pay 1.5X and international orders pay 2X shipping)	
CA Residents add 7.5% sales tax	
Total Payment in U.S. funds	$

❑ Check (Make checks payable to Mashiyach Press)
❑ Visa ❑ MasterCard ❑ AMEX
#_____
Expiration Date _____

Signature _____
Date_____

Visit our CyberNet-designed Web site: http://www.momentus.org/mash/